"**Warning!** Don't read this book if you have an open mind. Ben Radford goes beyond 'it's a mangy coydog' to explore an entirely new theory about the origins of the chupacabra phenomenon. My cryptozoological colleagues and fans, as well as the media, should read this one! I think Radford might be on to something! A fantastic read."

—**LOREN COLEMAN**, International Cryptozoology Museum,
author of *Bigfoot!*, *Cryptozoology A to Z*, and other books.

* * *

"**An amazingly thorough book**. . . . Having sequenced the DNA of three of the purported chupacabra beasts myself, I am impressed at the depth to which Radford delves into the backstory behind the chupacabra. Unlike the numerous uncritical popular writings about the chupacabra, Radford provides easy-to-read yet scholarly coverage of this subject."

—**TODD R. DISOTELL**, New York University

* * *

"*Tracking the Chupacabra* **combines detective work,** scientific analysis, and a keen sense of human psychology to unravel the mystery of the chupacabra. Radford provides the cultural context for the monster, and offers a comprehensive look at both the mythological and biological elements underlying the mystery. Ben Radford is at once sympathetic to and critical of the field of cryptozoology, and the field's practitioners would do well to follow his example of measured skepticism and commitment to science and reason. This is an engaging read that both scientists and the lay public will enjoy. Radford has slain the beast!"

—**DAVID DAEGLING**, University of Florida, author of *Bigfoot Exposed*

* * *

"**A wonderful adventure** into the quirky legend of our newest popular monster. Radford manages a very rare feat of balancing the excitement and magic of the monster hunt, with the rational skeptical approach of the scientist. I really enjoyed it."

—**STEPHEN ASMA**, Columbia College, Chicago, author of *On Monsters*

* * *

"Radford does a masterful job—part detective investigation, part anthropological analysis—of revealing the not-so-awful truth behind the chupacabra legend. In fact, Radford's deconstruction definitively and entertainingly sucks the mystery out of the poor old goatsucker."

—**KENNETH FEDER**, Central Connecticut University, author of *Frauds, Myths, and Mysteries: Science and Pseudoscience in Archaeology* and other books

* * *

"The most comprehensive dissection of the chupacabra phenomenon that I have ever read. Ben Radford leaves no stone unturned in his tenacious, unrelenting pursuit of precisely what is—and, more to the point, what is *not*—behind this veritable celebrity of modern-day cryptozoology. Is the chupacabra a bona fide mystery beast, or is it just a media-hyped monster of the imagination? Read this compelling book, which combines healthy skepticism with objective investigation throughout, and judge for yourself!"

—**KARL SHUKER**, author of *The Beasts That Hide from Man, Extraordinary Animals Worldwide*, and other books

* * *

"Radford goes after the chupacabra with the same kind of knowledge and energy that Dr. Van Helsing showed in pursuing Dracula in Bram Stoker's classic horror novel. Radford drives a metaphorical stake into the heart of the beast, reporting his investigations in lively prose, free of academic jargon yet rich with insights from folkloristics, biology, and psychology. Radford interviewed the eyewitnesses as well as reviewing the published and popular-culture descriptions of the chupacabra; then he applied scientific and folkloric analysis to the data. His conclusions—clearly and even humorously reported—provide the definitive word on this twenty-first-century vampire."

—**JAN HAROLD BRUNVAND**, University of Utah, author of *The Encyclopedia of Urban Legends, The Truth Never Stands in the Way of a Good Story*, and many other books

Tracking the Chupacabra

Tracking
the
Chupacabra

THE VAMPIRE BEAST IN FACT,
FICTION, AND FOLKLORE

Benjamin Radford

University of New Mexico Press   Albuquerque

LIBRARY OF CONGRESS CATALOGING-IN-PUBLICATION DATA

Radford, Benjamin, 1970–

Tracking the Chupacabra : the vampire beast in fact, fiction, and folklore / Benjamin Radford.

   p. cm.

Includes index.

ISBN 978-0-8263-5015-2 (pbk. : alk. paper)

1. Chupacabras. I. Title.

  QL89.2.C57R34 2011

  001.944—dc22

                    2010041879

TEXT: Minion Pro Regular, 10.25/14

DISPLAY TYPE: Cronos Pro

DESIGN AND LAYOUT: Melissa Tandysh

This book is dedicated to those for whom truth matters.

Contents

Acknowledgments

I would like to thank the following people for their support, ideas, and research assistance in slaying this vampire: Maya Elsner, Tom Flynn, Jenna Griffith, Jay Koester, Daniel Loxton, Blake Smith, David Sutton, and Jill Root. And, of course, The Mom and The Dad.

Thanks also to all the librarians, experts, and chupacabra eyewitnesses who shared their stories with me, including Jerry Ayer, Phylis Canion, and Madelyne Tolentino.

Introduction

I have investigated mysterious and unusual phenomena for over a decade, scientifically examining myriad claims from ghosts to crop circles, miracles to lake monsters. My research into the chupacabra spanned five years, taking me from dusty Texas towns to humid Central American jungles, from sunny Caribbean islands to harshly lit library archives. While some may think it was a fool's errand ("Why would you spend so much time and effort on the chupacabra?"), I believe it was time well spent, for solutions are always more valuable than mysteries. In any event, it was a fascinating journey.

On a final note, if I overexplain some concepts it is because I am keenly aware of how much misinformation there is about this subject, and I have erred on the side of caution. The issues can be complex and nuanced, and I hope readers will forgive any repetition.

PART I

THE SHORT HISTORY
OF THE CHUPACABRA

1

The Goatsucker Mystery

A mong the monsters said to roam the world's desolate deserts and dense jungles, perhaps none is more feared than the bloodthirsty chupacabra.[1] Rooted in conspiracy theory and anti-American sentiment, the chupacabra is a contradictory and bizarre amalgamation of vampiric monster, folk myth, and chameleon. It is a shapeshifter, changing its appearance and characteristics according to the time and place it is seen, and according to the beliefs and expectations of those who see it.

Bigfoot, the mysterious bipedal beast said to roam the North American wilderness, is named after what it leaves behind: big footprints. Bigfoot's Hispanic cousin, the chupacabra, is also known less for what it *is* than for what it leaves behind: dead animals. Though goats are said to be its favorite prey (*chupacabra* means *goat sucker* in Spanish), it has also been blamed for attacks on cats, sheep, rabbits, dogs, chickens, ducks, hogs, and other animals.

Descriptions of the chupacabra vary widely, but many accounts suggest that the creature stands about four to five feet tall. It has short but powerful legs that allow it to leap fantastic distances, long claws, and terrifying black or glowing red eyes. Some claim it has spikes down its back; others report seeing stubby, bat-like wings. Some say the stench of sulfur taints the air around chupacabras, or that it emits a terrifying hiss when threatened (see, for example, Carroll 2003).

While some mistakenly believe that chupacabra sightings date back to the 1970s, the chupacabra first gained real notoriety in 1995 in Puerto Rico. No one knew for certain why or how the chupacabra seemingly suddenly sprang into existence, but many Latin Americans believe it is the unholy creation of secret U.S. government experiments in the jungles of Puerto Rico. It had a heyday of about five years, when it was widely reported in Mexico, Chile, Nicaragua, Spain, Argentina, Brazil, and Florida, among other places.

The chupacabra can be categorized as appearing in three different physical forms (and countless cultural ones). The "original" and best known is that of a five-foot-tall bipedal creature with long claws and a distinctive row of spikes down its back, reported in August 1995 by Puerto Rican eyewitness Madelyne Tolentino. The second form is a mammal from the Canidae family, a small, four-legged beast looking very much like a dog or a coyote. The third is a catchall category that basically includes any unusual animal, alive or dead, that anyone reports seeing or thinks for whatever reason might be the dreaded chupacabra. This version of the chupacabra includes everything from a "kangaroo with wings" to a dried and misshapen ocean animal.

Whatever form it takes, in fifteen years it has become a global phenomenon—the world's third best-known monster (after Bigfoot and the Loch Ness Monster). In 2002, a writer for *Fortean Times* magazine ("Chupacabras Rides Agains Again" 2002a) noted that "[n]ot since the advent of crop circles has a strange phenomenon been so quickly assimilated into popular culture. Chupacabras is now equal to the Loch Ness Monster or Bigfoot as a cultural icon."

Some researchers, such as Loren Coleman and Scott Corrales, suggest that the name *chupacabras* dates back to 1960, when a character on the TV Western show *Bonanza* referred to a *chupacabras*. It seems that this reference was to a whippoorwill bird (*Caprimulgus vociferus*), which folklore suggested drank milk (not blood) from goats. Other than the shared name, however, there is no connection between the insect-eating whippoorwill bird and the Hispanic vampire beast *el chupacabra*. As Coleman (2010) notes, "the vampire element appears to be a recent addition to the folkloric aspects of these tales." (A "goat-sucker" is also referred to in the writings of Aristotle, though no serious researcher would suggest that the Greek philosopher, who died in 322 BC, was referring to the subject of this book.)

Confounding the Mystery

For a creature as well known as the chupacabra, it has been the subject of remarkably little serious research. Information on the beast is fragmentary, often poorly sourced, and contradictory. In the world of chupacabra, proven facts and wild speculations mix freely and indistinguishably. Researcher Karl Shuker (2009b) lamented the "immense confusion and contradiction" surrounding the chupacabra, making it "almost impossible to distinguish fact from fiction, and reality from hearsay and local lore" about the creature.

The chupacabra has of course made its way into various books on unexplained mysteries. While a few authors write with some scholarship and authority on the chupacabra, the vast majority of information on the subject is rife with error, mistaken assumption, and misinformation. Often this misinformation is because authors, instead of doing the "heavy lifting" of any actual investigation, fact-checking, or research, will simply copy liberally from other authors and other sources, sometimes embellishing or inventing facts along the way to spice up the story.

Listing all the instances of sloppy scholarship (enumerating mistakes and their corrections) would take a book in itself, but a few examples will set the stage. I expose some here and throughout the book, not necessarily to chide careless authors, but because it cannot be overemphasized just how shabby research on the chupacabra has been. This shabbiness is a direct cause of the seemingly hopeless welter of contradictions and confusions, and this book is in part an exercise in setting the record straight and debunking extraneous myths that only shroud the truth behind the goatsucker.[2]

Chupacabra Descriptions

When it comes to descriptions of the goatsucker, authors arbitrarily pick and choose which details they want to use to create their chimeric chupacabra. W. Haden Blackman, for example, in his *Field Guide to North American Monsters* (1998), states that the "typical chupacabra is covered in glossy matted hair and has a feral face. Its long limbs, which end in massive claws, can propel the monster across any terrain at amazing speeds, but it is the creature's powerful bat-like wings that allow it to migrate huge distances . . . Goatsuckers are deceptively small, standing just three to four feet high." George Eberhart's *Mysterious Creatures: A Guide to Cryptozoology* offers another description: "Height, four to five feet. Covered in short, gray fur. Said to have a chameleon-like ability to change color. Large, round head. Huge, lidless, fiery-red eyes run up to the temples and spread to the sides. Ears small or absent. Two small nostrils. Lipless mouth. Sharp, protruding fangs. Pointy spikes run from the head down the spine; these may double as wings. Thin arms with three webbed fingers. Muscular but thin hind legs. Three clawed toes. No tail" (Eberhart 2002,

106). Loren Coleman and Patrick Huyghe, in their *Field Guide to Bigfoot, Yeti, and Other Mystery Primates Worldwide* (1999), draw from the same chief eyewitness and offer a similar description, but curiously suggest the creature might be a type of freshwater merbeing.

The book *A Natural History of the Unnatural World* (written by the fictional Cryptozoological Society of London, ghostwritten by Joel Levy) states that the chupacabra is "a strange two-legged creature, about four to five feet high, which looked like a cross between an alien and a fanged kangaroo . . . it has sharp spines down its back, a powerful tail . . . and staring red eyes and big ears and needle-like teeth for the blood sucking" (Levy 1999). Not to be outdone, Giles Sparrow's *Field Guide to Fantastic Creatures* describes it as "a strange reptilian beast with a kangaroo-like gait, glowing red eyes and a row of sharp spines running along its back" (Sparrow 2009, 92–93). The beast is depicted with long, spindly limbs and four long-fingered claws on each hand. Another book states that the beast is "five feet tall with a pronounced lower jaw, large red eyes, small nostrils, and a razor-thin mouth with curved fangs. It has a rough black coat . . . Jagged spikes are said to grow on its back . . . it looks kind of like a dinosaur" (Genzmer and Hellenbrand 2007, 248–49).

From this sample we can see that, depending on which book you are reading (or whose eyewitness account you believe), the chupacabra either has a "powerful tail" or it has no tail at all; it either spends most of its time flying in the night skies—or doesn't, lacking wings. It might have three fingers on each hand, or four; it might have a row of distinctive spikes running down its back—or it might not. Its ears are either "big" or they are "small or absent." About the only detail these accounts have in common is the pair of red eyes. Remarkably, several writers (including Herbert Genzmer and Ulrich Hellenbrand, in their book *Mysteries of the World*) conclude that "[t]he descriptions are, for the most part, very similar"!

If these summaries of the chupacabra characteristics are confusing and contradictory, the original eyewitness descriptions (presented in later chapters) are even worse. The huge disparity in chupacabra reports is one of the things that Loren Coleman finds most fascinating. "It is intriguing that a relatively small number of sightings of an upright gray, spiky haired primate in Puerto Rico morphed into a widespread misidentification of four-legged, usually black and brown dogs, foxes, coyotes, and other canids with or without mange, living or dead, as chupacabras," he told me in an interview. But here we are getting ahead of the story; let's begin at the beginning, in Puerto Rico.

The Puerto Rican Chupacabra

The Puerto Rican chupacabra panic began in March 1995 when residents in the small towns of Orocovis and Morovis discovered farm animals that had apparently been drained of blood through small puncture wounds (Corrales 1996). Similar mysterious mutilations and desanguinations occurred occasionally around the island, but the creature or creatures responsible were rarely sighted. It seemed the elusive vampires somehow always managed to do their dirty work away from prying eyes. Puerto Rican comedian Silverio Perez claimed he coined the name *chupacabra* shortly after the first attacks became public (though others dispute this claim; Jonathan Downes, for example, states that his friend Ismael Aguayo came up with the monicker [2009]). Regardless of who named it, the act of labeling the chupacabra in a real way created the creature. The idea that *something* was attacking animals in Puerto Rico was not new, but the one-word label gave it a name, currency, and credibility—and soon dozens of eyewitnesses would give it dozens of different, chaotic forms.

About five months would pass before the first person actually caught a glimpse of the blood beast, in Canovanas, about twenty minutes east of the capital of San Juan. In fact, that eyewitness sighting provided much more than a glimpse; it was an incredibly thorough and detailed description of what would become the world-famous chupacabra. This sighting in turn spurred further reports and sightings. The tabloids and news media pounced on each new report as if it were catnip, eager to warn their audiences about this novel, bloodthirsty menace with sensational stories. It is against this background that the Puerto Rican chupacabra came into its own. Scott Corrales's 1997 book *Chupacabras and Other Mysteries* provides a fascinating glimpse into the origins of the chupacabra phenomenon in Puerto Rico. Of particular interest are the eyewitness descriptions, and the public's reactions to the creature.

Eyewitness Descriptions of the Puerto Rican Chupacabra

The book *Chupacabras and Other Mysteries* lists dozens and dozens of eyewitness reports and descriptions; here is a sample: "the thing was generally humanoid in appearance, three to four feet tall, and had orange-yellow eyes" (Corrales 1997, 14); "a round-headed creature with elongated black eyes, a fine jaw, and a small mouth, with chameleon-like pigmentation, alternating from purple to brown to yellow, while its face was a dark graying color" (15); "a gargoylesque creature" (15); "a creature between three and four feet tall, with the body and dense, black plumage of an eagle, a thick neck, piercing eyes, [and] a wolf-like muzzle instead of a beak" (23); a creature four feet tall that walked on two legs with "elongated red eyes, large fangs, claw-like hands, and a dark grey body" (119). Yet other eyewitnesses described a "creature with pointed ears, strange profile, and a shaven head" that "ran like a gazelle" (114); an animal "three feet tall, with a crest on its back, large wings, and three-fingered hands" (125); a "monster about 30 inches tall weighing 66 pounds, and having ashen-dark feathers and sizeable wings" (142). How this witness could provide such exacting height and weight measurements for the beast is a mystery in itself.

Karl Shuker, in his book *The Unexplained* (2009a), offers yet another amalgamated description: "Based upon a considerable corpus of eyewitness descriptions, the chupacabras seemingly stands 1–1.5 meters (3–5 feet) tall, with large slanted eyes (sometimes said to glow orange or red), and bare holes instead of lobed ears." One writer, Marc Davenport, stated that "several witnesses swore that the goatsucker's eyes emitted beams of light that illuminated nocturnal landscape like flashlight beams . . . Many who saw the chupacabras said it has a web of skin that connects its wrist to its knee or ankle, and this web forms a 'wing,' like that of a flying squirrel when it raises its arms, and that this structure allows it to glide like a hang glider. But some witnesses insisted that the chupacabra has a levitation capability that allows it to float through the air like Superman. One witness claimed that the extremely rapid movement of small, feather-like appendages along its backbone propelled it like a bumblebee" (Corrales 1997, 4).

At least one writer suggested that the chupacabra had language skills and could understand spoken Spanish (including profanities), as seen in this description of an eyewitness's encounter: "The housewife's eyes met those of the inhuman creature and stared it down, as she thought aloud, 'If you're the Chupacabras, you're a pretty sorry excuse for a creature,' then promptly added the abusive word *pendejo* to her thought. The gargoylesque entity slowly covered its pointed face with its wings, as if hurt by her rebuff. It moved away from its position, slinked against a wall, and half hid behind a washing machine" (Corrales 1997, 107).

Almost as bizarre as the reports of the chupacabra's visage were reports of its actions. A farmer named Rafael Morenowas claimed that a chupa cabra had taken sexual liberties with his cows. (Loren Coleman, in his 2003 book *Bigfoot!*, included reports of Bigfoot raping cows as well.) Some Puerto Ricans, borrowing from werewolf mythology, believed that only silver bullets would stop the chupacabra, and several Puerto Rican UFO groups claimed that the creature was the source of the AIDS epidemic. One group put forth the theory that the chupacabra "was one of twenty or more beings that had descended to Earth to conduct experiments with human blood in order to produce blood viruses aimed at eliminating humanity. This effort was supposed to depopulate the earth, leaving it open for alien colonization." Writer Scott Corrales dismisses such claims as wild, unfounded speculation—which indeed they are—but accepts many equally outlandish ideas and reports.

Wild speculation ran rampant throughout Puerto Rico at the height of the chupacabra hysteria. Many of the rumors and stories about the chupacabra were so wild that almost any story, no matter how outlandish, unfounded, or clearly wrong, would gain credence with someone somewhere. This social climate of few facts and sensationalist tabloid headlines combined with wild rumor and gossip to create a perfect breeding ground for a mild form of mass hysteria in which ordinary events (such as attacks by dogs on pets or livestock) were interpreted in extraordinary ways.

Madelyne Tolentino

Emerging from out of this confused welter of contradictory reports was the best chupacabra sighting in history, from a woman named Madelyne Tolentino. It is the most important chupacabra description on record, not only because of its detail but also because it is the "original" chupacabra description upon which the most famous depictions of the creature are based. As Scott Corrales notes, "The first descriptions of this mysterious creature came about six months into the mutilation epidemic. In September, sightings by Madelyne Tolentino, a housewife

Figure 1. The most popular depiction of the chupacabra, based on an eyewitness sighting by Madelyne Tolentino of Puerto Rico. Illustration by the author from a sketch by Jorge Martín.

of Canovanas—a city to the east of the island's capital, San Juan—and others gave it a form and a name" (Corrales 1996).

Tolentino said the chupacabra she saw had dark eyes that went up the temples and spread around the sides; it was about four feet high, walked like a human on two legs, and had thin arms and legs, with three fingers and toes at the end of each limb. It had no ears or nose, but instead two small airholes. She also noted what appeared to be feathers, spikes, or feathery spikes on the creature's back (fig. 1); much more on this topic later.

The Chupacabras Spread

Though the chupacabra had its heyday in the last half of 1995 and early 1996, the beast soon spread from its Puerto Rican home, looking for more goats to suck in the greener pastures of the mainland. As news stories of the chupacabra spread, so did the reported sightings of the creature. "The chupacabra craze had its own significance to the inhabitants of Canovanas who were at first flattered by the international attention they received; a mood which shifted to sour betrayal upon discovering just how quickly their narratives could escape their ownership and control" (Derby 2008, 292). In March 1996, Spanish language talk show host Cristina Saralegui, on her popular show *Cristina*, aired a story about the goatsucker, followed almost immediately by an increase in reports from Mexico and Spanish-speaking areas of the United States.

The chupacabra was reported in a dozen or so other countries—all of them, quite significantly, Spanish-speaking or Portuguese-speaking areas. A complete accounting of every single report would be both tedious and repetitive, but in the next sections I highlight some of the better-known, representative, and more revealing chupacabra reports outside of Puerto Rico after 1995. A close analysis of these reports reveals that the majority of them, though widely claimed to be "reports of the chupacabra" (and cited as evidence for the animal), in fact have no sighting of the goatsucker at all. Instead they are merely reports of animals mysteriously drained of blood and *assumed* to have been attacked by the beast. As we will see, there is not necessarily a cause-and-effect link.

Mexico

In north and central Mexico, especially in the state of Jalisco, sheep and goats were said to have been attacked by the chupacabra in May 1996. According to an Associated Press report (1996), "The dead animals all reportedly have two tooth marks about a third of an inch across in the neck and appear to have been drained of blood. Rumors of the attacks on livestock are roaring through Jalisco despite the official doubt and denial heaped upon them. Francisco Rodrigues Herrejon, director of the Guadalajara Zoo, took a cast of a pawprint and said it looked like that of a large dog or wolf."

Responding to a handful of early Mexican chupacabra reports, in April 1996 a team of scientific investigators in Mexico City, Patricia and Mario Mendez-Acosta, began a search for the beast. According to a report in *Skeptical Inquirer* magazine (Nickell 1996), the team "staked out farmyards where the goatsucker had reportedly struck. Wild dogs were caught each time. A police official remarked, 'I don't know about the rest of Mexico or the rest of the world, but here the goatsuckers are just dogs. There is this huge psychosis. You see it everywhere.'"

Reports of the Mexican chupacabra continued to surface occasionally, but grew rarer with each passing year. On Halloween 2001, a farmer in Chihuahua heard dogs on his ranch howling at around midnight; the next day, reports claimed, he found thirty-five of his sheep dead, and he claimed that they were entirely drained of blood from two small bite marks on their necks. He saw no chupacabra, but assumed it lurked nearby.

In March 2008 the chupacabra reappeared in the Champotón, Campeche, municipality. Eight hens and a turkey were killed when something "arrived and sucked the blood from them and later escaped without leaving a sign." Though no one got a good look at whatever attacked the animals, "neighbors said that it was the chupacabra, because the attack to the fowl had the same characteristics of when some years ago animal slaughters were reported in other parts of the country." The dead hens caused a panic among Champotón residents, who brought their livestock inside their homes for protection and formed an armed mob to hunt down the goatsucker: "a brigade crosses the streets by night, armed with poles and machetes to catch or kill the assumed chupacabra" (Ynurreta 2008). Nothing was ever found.

Chile

The chupacabra apparently traveled to the northern Chilean city of Calama in April 2000, where unverified reports said that as many as three hundred animals were found dead, at least some of them drained of blood. No one saw the attacks, but residents said they heard terrifying sounds in the night's darkness and were afraid to investigate until the next morning. Police searched the area, finding nothing but footprints.

Marc Herman, writing for Discovery.com, noted that "[u]ntil April of 2000, the beast had never ranged as far as Chile. Though attacks on live-stock are not unheard of around Calama, a rural community near a wilder-ness hosting pumas and smaller predators, the violent mystery caught the nation's fancy. Within days of the first reports, the attacks had become a media sensation, with headlines dominating the national press and amateur video of the slaughtered livestock playing every night on the local news" (Herman 2000).

The local governor, Francisco Segocia, called for an investigation and announced that "the footprints were taken to the Investigations lab. We can-not say what they are at this time, but at first sight, they come pretty near to dog prints, which tend to expand and acquire strange shapes. An operation has been conducted, and we want to point out that no evidence of the pres-ence of a strange animal was found" (Herman 2000). In June the investigation concluded that the animals were killed by feral dogs. Many in the public were skeptical of this explanation and smelled, if not the stench of a chupacabra, at least a government cover-up.

Though Chile cannot lay claim to having the most chupacabra reports in Iberoamerica, it does have the dubious distinction of being home to some of the most outlandish. Following the official report about the Calama preda-tion, newspapers ran articles by prominent Chilean UFO researchers who claimed that the military had found three chupacabra eggs in Chile's northern Atacama desert, and, through top-secret clandestine genetics experiments—in collaboration with the American government, of course—had hatched new chupacabras. Indeed, "The chupacabra material was then turned over to NASA, according to Chilean press accounts. Radio programs in Chile have also accused the American space agency of creating the chupacabra in a lab in the first place, while conducting genetic tests in the Chilean desert" (Herman 2000). In another variation of the story described on the website UnexplainedStuff.com, "Chilean soldiers had captured a chupacabra male, female, and cub that had been living in a mine north of Calama. Then, accord-ing to the account, a team of NASA scientists arrived in a black helicopter and reclaimed the chupacabra family. The creatures, so the story claimed, had escaped from a secret NASA facility in the Atacama Desert of northern Chile where the U.S. space agency was attempting to create some kind of hybrid beings that could survive on Mars" (UnexplainedStuff.com 2008).

In many cases in Chile and elsewhere, rumors of the chupacabra's presence were completely unrelated to any livestock deaths, mysterious or otherwise. For example, according to one television report, a taxi driver in the capital city of Santiago said that he saw "a strange winged beast, about the size of a man, running alongside his car as he drove home" one evening. The bizarre bipedal beast ran past his speeding car, and stories spread by the news media suggested he had seen the chupacabra. Then there's the report that a miner in the town of Huasco had captured a chupacabra that resembled a "kangaroo with wings." The beast, Chilean newspaper *Las Ultimas Noticias* reported in November 2001, had escaped the miner's captivity but had flown to a nearby mine, where police had the goatsucker cornered ("Chupacabras" 2002b). Perhaps not suprisingly, no further details were forthcoming.

These examples—and countless others—illustrate the danger in taking chupacabra reports at face value, even those not published in sensationalized tabloid newspapers. Proponents of the chupacabra's existence like to cite laundry lists of "sightings" and news reports about the goatsucker, as if the sheer quantity of them amounts to irrefutable evidence for the beast. Yet almost invariably most of the reports are either (1) patently fictional; or (2) so heavily sensationalized that there's no way to know what may have been actually sighted; or (3) sightings of some odd animal or monster that has nothing to do with the chupacabra or its signature form of vampiric predation; or (4) only mention dead livestock, with no clear connection to the chupacabra.

Brazil

On May 24, 1999, nine pigs on a farm in Sorocaba, Brazil, were found dead; according to one report in the *Estado de São Paulo* newspaper, "The bodies had been drained of blood and the predator left neither tracks nor signs of entering the locked enclosure. . . . Farm owner Celso Rabello, 47, believed the animals were victims of the mysterious chupacabras" ("Chupacabras Strikes Again" 1999). Though no mention is made of any necropsy done on any of the animals, Rabello allegedly stated confidently that "[t]he body didn't have a single spoonful of blood."

According to Joseph Trainor, editor of *UFO Roundup*, among some ranchers in the southern parts of Brazil (especially the states of Paraná and São Paulo) there exists a belief in an unknown, savage creature called O Bicho (the beast). Trainor reports several supposed encounters with O Bicho, including one incident in February 1997 when a ranch housekeeper named José Batista de Moraes heard loud noises coming from outside. "'When I approached the corral, I heard sheep bleating and a loud rumble, a type of growling that I'd never heard before,' Batista de Moraes said. 'I tried to enter through the gates, but they were tightly shut. By the time I got to the other gate, the strange animal had escaped.' Inside the corral, Batista de Moraes 'switched on the lights and found a scene of massacre. Twelve sheep lay dead, and another eleven were very much chewed up. All of the sheep were mutilated with surgical precision'" (Trainor 1997).

This final, mysterious detail—the wounds created with "surgical precision"—is a staple of supposed UFO-related cattle mutilations. (Note the contradiction in this account, with the sheep being both "very much chewed up" *and* their wounds "mutilated with surgical precision," as chewing or biting cannot create the clean cuts characteristic of "surgical precision.") Because no one gave a description of O Bicho (much less one that resembled a chupacabra), and there is no mention of vampirism in this account, despite the author's lumping O Bicho together with the goatsucker, there seems to be no real connection to the chupacabra. Similar stories appeared in Argentina in 2002 and 2005, often associated specifically with cattle mutilations. The "mystery" of cattle mutilations per se (absent vampirism or explicit chupacabra reports) is beyond the scope of this book, but I deal with the subject in some depth in chapter 8.

The United States

The chupacabra's first appearance in the United States was said to have been in Miami, Florida, on March 11, 1996, when it attacked some animals. Researcher Virgilio Sanchez-Ocejo of the Miami UFO Center took plaster casts of tracks left by the beast (fig. 2) and compared them to those he had taken from the chupacabra sightings in Calama, Chile. He concluded that the tracks belonged to an unknown, probably extraterrestrial, creature.

Experts, however, weren't so sure. In his book *The Island of Paradise*, Jonathan Downes described "a plastercast of a footprint that had been given to me in Miami during February 1998 by a well-meaning UFO expert who claimed that it had come from a chupacabra. The problem was that neither the footprint, nor the animal that the eyewitness who had originally procured the footprint claimed had made it, had anything to do with the chupacabra. . . . Although I am loathe to discount the matron's evidence of what

Figure 2. An alleged chupacabra track recovered in Florida. Photo by the author.

she saw, my footprint would not stand up in a court of law . . . Whatever the footprint is, it is certainly not that of a chupacabra" (Downes 2008b, 63).

Esteban Sarmiento, a primatologist and functional anatomist at the American Museum of Natural History, came to the same conclusion when he examined the tracks provided by Sanchez-Ocejo for a 2005 television documentary. He found clear evidence of hoaxing, concluding that the tracks were either sculpted or the animal that made the print was being held and pushed down in the dirt to make the cast. "Just on the evidence of this cast, which doesn't have much credibility, I wouldn't believe the animal exists," Sarmiento concluded (*Is It Real?* 2005). Whether Sanchez-Ocejo faked the chupacabra track or was himself the victim of a prank is unclear, but either way it seems hoaxing was afoot.

One of the stranger American reports of the chupacabra came from a young Hispanic boy in suburban Tucson, who told his father, José Espinoza, that a chupacabra opened the front door to their home, slammed the door behind it, walked through the kitchen, and sat on the boy's bed before jumping out a window. He described it as three feet tall, with long arms, no legs, a "beak," and a bright red nose (Valdez 1997; Corrales 1997, 130). No evidence was ever found of this creature. The case was profiled on the mystery-mongering television show *Animal X*. The show, known for its shoddy scholarship, stated that "[a] police investigation into the incident found the son's description consistent with previous sightings" (*Animal X* 1997). In fact, this "chupacabra" is completely unlike any other previous sightings, and was probably a hoax or the child's overactive imagination.

Olimpia Govea of Sweetwater, Florida, claimed that twenty-seven chickens and two goats had been killed by the chupacabra. When professionals from the local zoo explained that her animals were likely killed by roving dogs, Govea ridiculed the experts: "If dogs were to blame, she challenged, why didn't they feast on the kill—and more importantly, what kind of dog leaves no blood behind at the scene of the carnage?" (Corrales 1997, 129). Govea's indignant response is typical of many people who believe their animals were killed by the goatsucker; she had suffered a scary shock (not to mention a monetary loss), and felt that she was being ignored and patronized by arrogant experts who dismissed her claims and discounted her experience.

Govea's response is also typical in that she is simply mistaken about what canid predation looks like (see chapter 8). Both feral dogs and coyotes exist in Florida—in fact the official website of the city of St. Petersburg, Florida, even provides information for its residents about coyote attacks on pets and livestock ("Florida Coyote" 1998). Accurate information on canine predation can be found in the U.S. Fish and Wildlife report *Procedures for Evaluating Predation on Livestock and Wildlife*, which states, "Domestic dogs can be a serious problem where they are permitted to run at large, particularly near urban areas" (Wade and Bowns 1984).

Why didn't they feast on the kill? Govea demanded. "Domestic dogs do not normally kill for food . . . As a rule, domestic dogs feed very little on their prey" (Wade and Bowns, 1984). Why was there little or no blood? Govea wanted to know. Since the animals were never taken for veterinary necropsy, there is no reason to think that the animals were drained of blood. Furthermore, since the dogs merely killed their prey (with a characteristic bite to the neck) and did not try to eat the animals, we would not expect a bloody scene. Govea's unfamiliarity with the signs of canid predation created a mystery where none existed. Once she (incorrectly) assumed that her animals had been visited by a vampire, she assumed the culprit was the chupacabra she'd heard about in newspapers, on the radio, and on television.

Theories about the Chupacabra's Origin

Though Puerto Rico, and the rest of the world, now had a name and a somewhat definitive description of the chupacabra, its origin was as puzzling as ever. Some believe the monster was left behind by visiting extraterrestrials; others think it is the result of top-secret U.S. government genetics experiments. Some of a deeply religious bent see the hand of Satan in the monster's work.

What do some of the top chupacabra researchers think about the animal? Though up until now there has been very little skeptical or scientific analysis of the chupacabra claims, a handful of experts have researched the subject. Scott Corrales, who has written more on the subject than anyone else, refused several requests to be interviewed for this book. Karl Shuker seemed to be more reserved than Corrales about the likelihood of the chupacabra's existence. He told me, "I think it possible that there is some unusual animal at the basis of at least some reports, but nothing remotely as exotic as the press would like to make out, and quite possibly comprising a situation where a host of wholly different entities are all being lumped together to create what is essentially a nonexistent composite. That is, the chupacabra as such is a created media monster made up of bits and pieces extracted from a welter of heterogeneous reports describing several totally unrelated animals" (Shuker 2009b).

Is a chupacabra responsible for most or all of the deaths attributed to it? No one disputes that many pets, livestock, and other animals have been killed by other animals in Puerto Rico and elsewhere; their carcasses stand as mute testimony to that reality. The real question is *what* creature killed them: something known and normal (such as a dog, coyote, or mongoose), or something unknown and possibly paranormal (such as a chupacabra)?

One way to approach the question is by first noting that livestock predation by normal animals is a proven fact. It is well known and beyond dispute that (depending upon the ecology of a specific geographic region) there may be dozens of animals that can—and do—attack animals such as geese, ducks, goats, cats, dogs, chickens, rabbits, cattle, and every other animal upon which the chupacabra is said to have preyed. Even animals that might not otherwise be aggressive can be pushed by environmental pressures to attack animals they would not ordinarily prey on for their very survival. Livestock predation has been a threat since humans first began domesticating animals millennia ago; this predation is nothing new or unusual.

Centre for Fortean Zoology researcher Jon Downes attributes at least some of the original Puerto Rican chupacabra reports to starving mongooses. He explains that in the early 1990s the island experienced an explosion in the rat population. As the rats became more common, the population of their chief predator, the mongoose, also jumped. After a while, having more mongooses solved the rat problem, but created another issue. With few natural predators and a dwindling rat population upon which to feed, the animals began starving, becoming more aggressive and attacking animals they had previously ignored: domestic creatures such as chickens, goats, and other livestock. This situation, Downes believes, explains many of the chupacabra victims having been "mysteriously" attacked: "I am certain that mongooses did the vast majority of the killings of domestic livestock" (Downes 2008b).

As support for this theory, he states, "the fact is that there haven't been any more killings since 1998, ten years now—and I have kept in touch with my people on the island and there still haven't—would suggest that the explosion in the rat population was the case, and the mongoose levels would return to normal again." While hardly definitive proof, Downes's theory seems to make sense from a zoological standpoint, and may in fact be true. (For his part, Loren Coleman offered reserved support for the mongoose explanation, telling me, "It is a theory that may explain part of what was occurring" [Coleman 2009].)

Puerto Rican zoologist Edwin Velasquez researched chupacabra claims, concluding that the so-called mysterious killings were attributable to dogs and mongooses. Another explanation is rhesus monkeys (*Macaca mulatta*), which have lived on the island for over thirty years. It seems that the monkeys had been introduced to the island for research purposes, and some had escaped and begun their own colony. Some of them may have attacked livestock and house pets.

Historically there seems no evidence of any unusual vampiric animals in Puerto Rico, confirming that the chupacabra is indeed of recent vintage. An 1830 report by a British army general described the island's generally favorable climate and lack of dangerous animals (except voracious rats): "There are no venomous snakes or reptiles, no beast of prey, no noxious bird, or insect . . . Puerto Rico also bears no resemblance to the other islands with respect to birds and other animals. There are neither monkeys nor rabbits, nor any of the innumerable classes of quadrupeds and birds to be found in the immense forests of South America. But rats of an enormous size, and in great numbers, infest the country, and sometimes commit great ravages . . ." (Flinter 1834, 53).

So animal predation is not new. What is new and unusual—so the chupacabra proponents claim—is the element of vampirism, the hundreds of carcasses allegedly mysteriously drained of every drop of blood. Certainly there exist vampiric animals such as vampire bats, leeches, lampreys, bedbugs, and mosquitoes. But none of these known vampires could be responsible for taking down even small rodents, much less goats and sheep. There must be something else at work. The chupacabra—unlike Bigfoot or the Loch Ness monster—is, at its little black heart, a vampire, and to understand it we must examine the vampire traditions from which the goatsucker is drawn.

PART II

FOLKLORE OF THE CHUPACABRA

2

A Brief History of Vampires

I n the West, when most people think of vampires, either historical (such as, supposedly, Romanian prince Vlad Țepeș) or literary (creations by Bram Stoker, Anne Rice, Stephen King, Stephenie Meyer, and countless others), the vampire they are familiar with has Slavic origins. Yet as a cultural entity, vampires are a worldwide phenomenon (Bullard 2000; Beresford 2008). The ancient Greeks wrote of vampires (or *vrykolakas*), malevolent undead creatures that stalked the living, bringing death and disease. Humans could become vrykolakas in several ways, for example if the person led a sinful life, was buried in unconsecrated ground, or was excommunicated.

The vampires most people are familiar with are revenants—a folkloric term meaning human corpses that are said to return from the grave to harm the living. Other, older versions of the vampire (from Greece, India, Egypt, Norse mythology, etc.) were not thought to be human at all but instead supernatural—possibly demonic—entities that were never human and therefore did not take human form when they stalked their prey (Beresford 2008, 22). Indeed, "though the word *vampire* did not enter the English language until 1732 (and so in effect prior to this point there were no 'vampires' per se), it is impossible to deny that early demons and revenants are precursors of the [modern] vampire" (Beresford 2008, 195). The chupacabra is just this sort of vampire.[1]

Paul Barber, author of *Vampires, Burial, and Death*, notes that the idea of some people returning from the dead and sucking blood or bodily sustenance is universal. Stories from nearly every continent and every culture have some localized version of the vampire, and "bear a surprising resemblance to the European vampire" (Barber 1988, 2).

From a folkloric perspective, vampires have many characteristics, including eternal life, shapeshifting, aversion to mirrors or sunlight, and so on. Vampire mythology is incredibly rich and far beyond the scope of this book, but I will focus on perhaps the two most important and distinctive elements of vampirism: (1) vampires draining blood, energy, or other bodily substance through physical contact (such as a touch or bite); and (2) vampires being blamed for unexpected deaths or unexplained misfortune.

"Europeans of the early 1700s showed a great deal of interest in the subject of the vampire," Paul Barber tells us, and begins his survey of vampirism with one of the first and most complete accounts of European vampires, a man named Peter Plogojowitz, from 1725:

> After a subject by the name of Peter Plogojowitz had died, ten weeks past . . . and had been buried according to the Raetzian custom, it was revealed that in this same village of Kisilova, within a week, nine people, both young and old, died also, after suffering a twenty-four-hour illness. And they said publicly, while they were yet alive, but on their death-bed, that the above-mentioned Plogojowitz, who had died ten weeks earlier, had come to them in their sleep, laid himself on them, and throttled them, so that they would have to give up the ghost.

These deathbed claims of nine people that Plogojowitz had come to them in a dream—and soon fell deathly sick—so alarmed the villagers of Kisilova that they soon marched to Plogojowitz's grave to exhume his body. The farmers and villagers all well knew the signs of vampires, told in hushed voices behind closed doors: an intact body, beard and nails still growing, and so on. They resolved to dig up Plogojowitz to see if he might be the cause of the mysterious deaths. Indeed, as the 1734 account reveals, a vampire was found:

> The hair and beard—even the nails, of which the old ones had fallen away—had grown on him; the old skin, which was somewhat whitish, had peeled away, and a fresh one had emerged under it. The face, hands, and feet, and the whole body were so constituted, that they could not have been more complete in his lifetime. Not without astonishment, I saw some fresh blood in his mouth, which, according to common observation, he had sucked from the people killed

Figure 3. Europeans unearth the body of a suspected vampire and stake its remains. From a lithograph by Louis-Pierre Rene de Moriane in *Tribunaux secrets,* 1864.

by him. In short, all the indications were present that such people [vampires] are said to have. (Barber 1988, 6)

This account is remarkable for its depth of historical detail, though not for the rarity of its occurrence. It was only one of hundreds, perhaps thousands, of similar events that occurred in Europe in the Middle Ages. The accounts follow a consistent and predictable pattern: Some unexplained misfortune befalls a person, family, or town—perhaps a drought dried up the crops, or an invisible, infectious disease struck down a community. Maybe malnutrition or disease caused a spate of unexpected stillbirths, or livestock fell to lightning or marauding prey. Any damaging event for which there was not any clear and obvious cause might be blamed on a vampire (Stein 1996, 779). Vampires are one "easy" answer to humanity's age-old question: why do bad things happen to good people?

This is a textbook example of what psychologists call magical thinking: people experience something bad that they do not understand, and search for possible causes. In modern times, superstitious thinking is treated as a peccadillo or with mild embarrassment, as when a gambler clears his throat twice for good luck before throwing dice in a game of craps, or a tennis player carefully avoids walking on the court's painted lines during a changeover. But superstition can have a far darker and graver side when people reach for supernatural explanations for things they do not understand. (For more on superstition and magical thinking, see Beyerstein 2007; Shermer 1997; and Vaughn 2008.)

A nearly identical process occurred with many witchcraft accusations, both in Europe and in America (Hill 1997; Roach 2002). An outsider, often a woman, might be blamed for some malefic event, and be rumored or imagined to posses some extraordinary ability. In the case of accused vampires, of course, the victims were already dead and suffered damage only to their desecrated corpses and their family's reputations. Witches, on the other hand, were often put on trial, burned alive, drowned, or crushed under rocks.

Paul Barber's book is a fascinating examination of how superstitious people came to believe that the vampire was active among them. He explains how ordinary people jumped to conclusions, essentially creating vampires where none existed—or perhaps more accurately, erroneously putting a specific face and form to universal and ancient preexisting notions about vampires. Barber also explains how ordinary decomposition processes were mistaken for unusual or supernatural phenomena. For example, though a layperson might assume that a body would decompose immediately, if the coffin is well sealed and airtight, putrefaction might be delayed by weeks or months; intestinal decomposition creates bloating that can force blood up into the mouth, making it look like a dead body has recently sucked blood (this appearance is especially likely if someone tries to drive a stake through the corpse's chest). These processes are well understood by doctors, morticians, and forensic pathologists, but not necessarily by the average person. The myriad processes are too detailed (and too gruesome) to go into here, but Barber's book is a bloody good read.

The case of presumed and "proven" vampire Peter Plogojowitz gives insight into what will become a very familiar pattern of vampirism and chupacabra claims: some unknown vampire being blamed for causing deaths and sucking blood from the victims, often based on myths and leaps of logic.

African Vampires

Though Europe is the continent best known for its vampires, an interesting history of vampire stories and legends arose in Africa during and after colonialism. Anthropologist Luise White, in her book *Speaking with Vampires:*

Rumor and History in Colonial Africa (2000), investigated stories of vampires throughout East Africa, particularly Kenya, Uganda, and Zambia. She found that people across many cultures, countries, and languages told similar stories (with localized variants) of vampires that sucked the blood out of ordinary, "common folk" Africans.

These vampires (known variously as *mumiami, banyama, wazimamoto,* and other names) were said to work in positions of power, such as the fire brigade or the police. They would roam the streets looking for victims to abduct and drain blood from. Sometimes they wore black overalls and carried buckets of blood; other times they drove gray or black trucks or Land Rovers devoid of lights or windows. Others claimed that victims were not snatched from the street but instead captured in specially prepared pits, either with police, firefighters, or prostitutes as accomplices. One informant from Kampala, Uganda, stated, "Whites are a really bad race . . . they used to keep victims in big pits . . . blood would be sucked from those people until they were considered useless . . . the victims were fed really good food to make them produce more blood . . . the job of the police recruit was to get victims and nothing else . . ." (White 2000, 37).

Significantly, these stories of the white vampires began between 1918 and 1925. There seem to be no stories of vampires (or at least not ones specifying that the vampires were white) before colonialism, though earlier invaders such as Arabs "were said to have killed Africans for the blood, which they made into medicine that they drank or smeared on their weapons." Furthermore, "Stories about white people taking precious fluids from the peoples they colonized were common in the eighteenth and nineteenth centuries" (17). These vampire stories endured and thrived for decades: "Between the mid-1920s and the mid-1950s, charges that Africans working for Europeans captured other Africans for their blood were commonplace" in countries like Rhodesia (181). Indeed, African belief in magic and vampires continues to this day (Radford 2010c). The chupacabra, however, is not a Slavic vampire, nor an African one; it is a uniquely Hispanic one.

Latin American Vampires

Seen in its cultural and historical context, it was inevitable that the vampire would appear in Latin America. Researcher Robert Jordan notes that "Latin American society is already one known for its propensity for religious superstition and the prevalence of supernatural events such as miracles, spiritual visions, sightings of the Virgin Mary, Satan, etc." (2008). Indeed, as Jonathan Downes has noted, "Puerto Rico is a land where monsters are commonplace" (2009), and in fact "strange animals are a well-known part of the island's culture. *Vejigantes*—papier mâché masks worn during the carnival—are the island's most popular crafts. Tangles of menacing horns, fang-toothed leering expression, and bulging eyes of these half-demon, half-animal creations makes these masks frightening, particularly at night . . . In Puerto Rico the tradition of the demon parade was combined with the masked ceremonies of Africa as figures of resistance against colonialism and imperialism" (Downes 2008, 32).

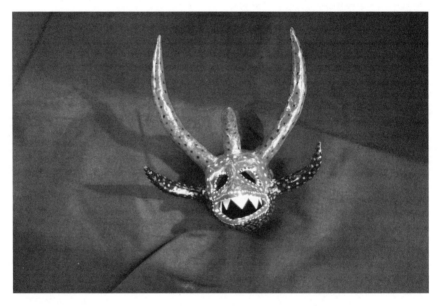

Figure 4. A *vejigante* mask used in Puerto Rican festivals. The grotesque, demonic masks were, according to lore, originally worn in public to scare sinners into attending church. Photo by the author.

Folklorist Thomas Bullard suggests that "[f]olk traditions in [Latin America] indicate that the chupacabra stories flourished not by accident but by a long acceptance of vampire-like activity—that this latest monster simply thrived in soil already fertilized by expectation. Christian and pagan elements of European, African, and New World origin have blended over the past 400 years into a vampire faith as vigorous as any in Eastern Europe, yet unexpected in spite of lying so close to home" (2000). Indeed, Bullard notes, "the Aztec civilization ran on blood. Religious practice centered on human sacrifice escalated to an industrial scale," with blood sacrifices routinely numbering in the hundreds and thousands. Anthropologist Nathan Wachtel notes of many Latin American cultures, "In the Andean world, blood and fat are among the essential offerings to the sacred powers: the sacrifice of slaughtered animals and the offering of their blood constitute the opening sequence of all religious ceremonies" (Wachtel 1994, 73).

Latin America, like many postcolonial societies, also endured a very real historical vampirism as Europeans took what they wanted and left the rest. This wholesale and often brutal extraction—of mountains of gold from the Aztecs by Hernán Cortés and his conquistadores in 1520; of rubber from Brazil's Amazon rainforest by British explorer Henry Wickham in 1876; of quinine from the Quechua Indians of Peru and Bolivia in the 1800s, the list goes on—has not been forgotten. The perception and resentment of having native resources taken by outsiders are very much a part of the Latin American cultural and social fabric.

Likichiri: Vampires of the Andes

Rumors of organ theft are common in Central and South America—often directed against Americans—but are not the only tales of vampirism. The likichiri, said to haunt the altiplano (highlands) of the Andes mountains, is another. Likichiri means "fat stealer" in Aymara, one of the prominent indigenous groups of the Andes. It is a well-known figure among the Quechua, Aymara, and other native groups. According to Eulogio Chavez, an ethnolinguist at the Ethnology and Folklore Museum in La Paz, Bolivia, the likichiri attacks people as they sleep. The fat thief cuts long, thin slits in the victims' sides and removes their fat. The extraction is painless, and the wound promptly heals without the victim's being any the wiser (Radford 1996; Ansion 1989). While at first this may seem like a cheap and efficient method of weight loss, the eventual results are much graver: unless treatment is given promptly, the victim will die. Treatments include the clandestine administration of a potion called achacachi, or, according to other sources, a black sheep's stomach membrane may be used. While the extraction of fat may seem trivial, it is important to realize that in the Andean highlands, fat helps keep people insulated and alive. Anyone left in the cold of the rugged mountain areas without protection, including natural body fat, is indeed in real danger.

Stories of vampiric creatures date back as early as the sixteenth century. Spanish historian Cristobal de Molina reported in 1571 that rumors circulated among Indians of the central Andes that the Spanish had arrived in Peru seeking not gold but human fat. The fat, they believed, was exported to Europe and used to cure specific diseases. The belief was so strong and widespread that "[t]he terrified Indians avoided all contact with the white men, refused to serve them, and went into hiding. They dared not enter the homes of the Spanish for fear of being killed, once inside, for their fat." Furthermore, this vampire "appears for the first time, historically, in the context of a profound crisis in the indigenous society and a movement to reject colonial domination" (Wachtel 1994, 75).

Since that time, the vampire's legend has clearly been updated. Most reported attacks occur in the mountains and high plains, but people are also said to be attacked in the cities as well. In La Paz, Bolivia's capital and largest city, hapless bus riders are said to be attacked late at night. Supposedly one can avoid being a likichiri victim by traveling only during the day, not walking alone at night, and eating garlic, which supposedly dilutes fat, making it less appealing or unusable to the likichiri. Carrying a mule bone is also supposed to help keep the bearer from falling asleep and becoming prey.

Although some sources claim that the likichiri is a spirit or an imaginary person, most people in La Paz, including Eulogio Chavez, believe it is a real person, or group of people, who have special abilities. Such abilities include the ability to put their victims to sleep, make the painless surgical incisions, and so on. Note that many of the powers ascribed to the likichiri are not necessarily assumed to be supernatural; many people today believe that hypnosis, for example, can make others fall asleep at will or dull the pain of a cut. The likichiri, then, is more like a vocation than a monster. "It's not necessarily evil," Chavez told me, "but a profession. It's an economic question" (Chavez 1996).

Unlike tales of native children's organs being harvested for implantation in rich foreigners' children (Radford 1999), the likichiri supposedly sells the fat he collects to international corporations—mostly American corporations—to be used for various purposes, including plastic surgery and the development of anesthetics. Unscrupulous company representatives buy the fat from the likichiri, knowing that it was taken from innocent Latin American victims.[2]

Similar urban legends elsewhere in the region include the *pishtacos* and the *sacaojos* ("eye-stealers") of Peru. In the case of the sacaojos, rumor spread in the Peruvian capital city of Lima that bands of foreigners had taken to the streets to kidnap children, later throwing them back on the pavement with their eyes gouged out. The eyes were said to be sold overseas at a lucrative profit.

When the chupacabra takes the life of valuable livestock animals it not only drains the blood, but by extension the money, opportunity, and livelihood of poor ranchers and farmers. In the likichiri legend, the very bodies of the native population are being taken from them. This theft fuels xenophobia and, indeed, "the figure of the Pishtaco is first of all that of a foreigner. This tall white—who drinks milk and sleeps by day—goes out at night carrying under his long coat a long knife with which he cuts up Indians. He uses their fat to oil his machines and their blood to sell to blood banks" (Shakespeare 1989, quoted in Campion-Vincent 1990). Indeed, "the likichiri generally appears with the features of a gringo, the diabolical incarnation of the outside world" (Wachtel 1994, 53).

Foreigners are occasionally accused of being likichiri and attacked. In 1983 a man was accused of being a vampire in the town of Orinoca; he was burned alive and his ashes scattered to the winds to prevent him from returning from the grave. One vampire incident in 1978 Bolivia bears a remarkable resemblance to reports of European vampires nearly 250 years earlier. French anthropologist Nathan Wachtel, who spent many years in the Bolivian Andes and had firsthand experience with accusations of modern-day vampires, described a vampire rumor that circulated in the town of Chipaya: "In 1978 many Chipayas had been stricken with a strange illness, characterized by sudden fatigue, a state of prostration from which many died. Suspicious-looking spots were found on the bodies of the sick (on their arms and chests), little dots that seemed to have been caused by the pricks of a needle: these traces clearly demonstrated that they had been victims of a *kharisiri* [vampire]" (Wachtel 1994, 54).

Recall that the local version of the vampire, the kharisiri (or likichiri), attacks its victims not with fangs but instead uses needles to drain the blood or fat from its victims. Thus the "needle-like spots" (whatever they were) were interpreted as the equivalent of two bite marks that one might expect to see on the neck of a victim of a European vampire—or, on the tropical island of Puerto Rico, "mysterious" puncture wounds on livestock. The man who was accused of being the vampire escaped with his life—but just barely. He was seized by a mob, tortured in an effort to make him divulge his accomplices, and finally thrown in jail for his own protection. His family was persecuted and ostracized, and his young children beaten to the point of retardation

(Wachtel 1994, 59–65). Perhaps significantly, the chief persecutor and "among the most unrelenting accusers" of the alleged vampire was one of the most prominent members of the local Pentecostal church.

Sporadic reports of vampires have continued. In 1987 a young merchant from the town of Huancayo, Peru, was accused of being a likichiri and lynched. In November 1988, in the capital city of Lima, "a rumor spread that gringos [white Europeans] dressed in white smocks and armed with machine guns were driving around the city streets scouting for children, their vehicle equipped with medical instruments that enabled them to tear out eyes (in addition to hearts or kidneys, according to certain versions), because of the need to export organs for transplants to 'pay foreign debts' . . . the ensuing mass hysteria brought about several attempted lynchings [including] of three young French tourists" (Wachtel 1994, 85).

Despite many inescapable similarities to the vampire legend (such as attacks that occur at night, the use of garlic to prevent attack, the draining of a bodily substance, ability to put others to sleep and turn invisible, etc.), Bolivian folklorist Eulogio Chavez sees no parallels between the two: "One is fiction," he told me. "The other occurs right here." Belief in vampires is not merely a quaint relic from the 1700s; it exists throughout Latin America and other places to this day.

Elsewhere in the Caribbean, not far from Puerto Rico's beaches, another vampire tradition exists: Haiti's *Loup Garou*, a werewolf that in some variants is also a vampire. As one researcher put it, "In voodoo-ridden Haiti, most of the population . . . trembles with fear at stories of witchcraft and vampires-cum-werewolves" (Woodward 1979, 150). Allowing for some hyperbole, there is much truth to this statement. In his 1959 book *Voodoo in Haiti*, Alfred Métraux recounted his experience on the superstition-soaked island: "At Maribal my friends gave me, in confidence, the names of all the werewolves in the district. . . . In 1948 several families lodged complaints with the *Chef de Section* [local police chief] against such and such a neighbour, accusing her of being the werewolf who has come to 'drain' (*secher*) their sick children" (Métraux 1959).

The Bloodsucking White Ogre

Folklorist Veronique Campion-Vincent, in discussing stories and legends of organ theft in Latin America, notes that "[t]he theme of the white ogre—of the malevolent white man endowed with somewhat supernatural attributes who needs blood or organs from the colored people whom he dominates—has been noted by many anthropologists in several third world regions. These anthropologists have found, often to their utter surprise, that they were assumed to be consumers of African blood, which they needed to survive. . . . The white ogre is very much alive in the Andean region of Latin America" (Campion-Vincent 1990, 19); for more on this, see Campion-Vincent 1997.

While the chupacabra is not necessarily interchangeable with the American "white ogre" metaphor in this respect, one of the most widespread theories about the monster's origin is that the U.S. government specifically (not the Canadians or Italians or other governments) created the chupacabra in an evil, clandestine genetics experiment gone horribly wrong. Thus in the minds of many Hispanics and Latin Americans, the chupacabra very much represents the United States. If America is the arrogant, paternalistic Dr. Frankenstein, the chupacabra is its unholy, bloodthirsty progeny.

The Puerto Rican Vampire

Vampires were, and are, very much a part of Puerto Rican culture and society. This is not to suggest that Puerto Ricans as a whole necessarily believe that actual, literal Dracula-vampire creatures stalk their island by night. Instead, residents of the U.S. territory feel that their cultural and social riches have been exploited and taken from them—often by external forces including the U.S. government. The vampires may be metaphorical, but they are no less real.

Resentment, distrust, and suspicion of the government are deeply embedded in Puerto Rican culture. Puerto Rico exists in some ways as the neglected child of the United States, not important enough to be its own state, yet apparently critical to the U.S. military for its war games and live fire exercises, especially on the island of Vieques—a sore point with thousands of locals who endured months of disruptive and potentially dangerous nearby artillery bombardments.

Resentment against the U.S. government comes from many quarters, including those unhappy about the island's being used as a junkyard for the Pentagon's toxic and radioactive depleted uranium-tipped ammunition, or their jungle at one point a testing ground for Agent Orange before its use in Vietnam (Jordan 2008). Such grievances run deep and bitter among many Puerto Ricans, who feel used and neglected. As one Puerto Rican told me, "Since we're not a state, they [the U.S. government] can do anything they want, and we have no power or status."

Sometimes this resentment is manifested in a sense of being preyed upon, and the vampirism metaphor is quite apt. The feeling of exploitation by larger and more powerful countries dates back centuries; a report from 1830 stated, "It is distressing to see the houses of all the inhabitants, even in the interior of the country, adorned with chairs and tables of foreign manufacture, and made of wood which in general is neither beautiful nor durable. The virgin forests of Puerto Rico are full of beautiful and durable wood of various kinds—which is exported, and is highly esteemed in foreign countries for furniture" (Flinter 1834, 135). It was not just wood; many of Puerto Rico's native resources (including cattle, coffee, sugar, and tobacco) were drained from the island and shipped off by and to foreigners.

Over a century later, there were "secret negotiations between highly popular governor Luis Muñoz Marin and Robert McNamara over the proposed removal of every last inhabitant of Vieques and Culebra and even their cemeteries" (Derby 2008, 308). Writer Robert Jordan notes that "[t]hese negotiations were code-named 'Plan Dracula,' or the Dracula Plan by Puerto Rican officials because U.S. officials insisted that all bodies from cemeteries be exhumed and relocated elsewhere upon U.S. purchase of the land. This early association of the U.S. government with a blood-sucking monster seems rather prophetic, and certainly could have played a role in the eventual characterization of the negative U.S. presence on the island as the chupacabra creature" (2008, 14).

Little wonder then that when some ranchers and farmers began reporting actual, literal vampire attacks, sporadically before 1995 and somewhat more regularly after August 1995—with real loss of blood, albeit from livestock and animals instead of peasants or children—the stories were met with some credulity. In a land where vampirism was perceived to take many forms, literal blood may have seemed an unsurprising next step.

The Vampire of Moca and the "Monster-Thing" of Nebraska

By 1995 Puerto Ricans were primed not only for a metaphorical vampire, but a literal one. Some twenty years before the chupacabra first reared its ugly head, the island was gripped by another vampire. In February and March 1975, stories circulated in the town of Moca that some unknown beast had attacked livestock and domestic animals (two ducks, a hog, three goats, and a pair of geese). "There was no trace of blood in any of the animals, in spite of the fact that the dead geese had snow-white feathers, upon which the slightest speck of blood would have showed up immediately," wrote one reporter (Corrales 1997). According to sociologist Robert Bartholomew, "Residents claimed that they heard loud screeches and/or flapping wings coinciding with the attacks. Academics and police examined the carcasses and blamed everything from humans to snakes to vampire bats" (2001, 17). The creature became known as "the Vampire of Moca." The claimed blood loss was never verified, and it seems the vampire did not strike again. This has been claimed by some to be one of the earliest reports of the chupacabra, but it seems very unlikely, for a number of reasons. First, it is not the first example of "mysterious" predation in Puerto Rico; second, if the Moca Vampire and the chupacabra are the same animal, then it is hard to understand the creature's twenty-year fast between meals. It makes no sense that a "goatsucker" would kill a handful of animals with perhaps a gallon of blood between them and then vanish for twenty years before suddenly reappearing and deciding to resume its quest for blood. Furthermore, according to Puerto Rican researcher Lucas Montes, the Moca animal killings were the work of local pranksters.[3]

In fact, a nearly identical "chupacabra" incident occurred a year before the Moca Vampire, in America's heartland. Dead cattle were said to be discovered with parts of their anatomy missing and mysterious blood loss in Nebraska and South Dakota in the fall of 1974 (Stewart 1977). Eyewitnesses reported seeing "a monster-thing," presumably having attacked the cattle and drained their blood. The creature "was described by the few persons who allegedly observed it as a hairy creature that walked on all fours and quickly vanished when seen by humans. All sightings took place at night and not one actually got a good look at the animal." Farmers and ranchers demanded to know what unknown monster was preying on their livestock, but there were no clues, not even footprints. (I examine this case in more depth in chapter 8.) Some researchers claim that the chupacabra (or another unknown vampiric creature) attacked Puerto Rican livestock prior to the 1970s, but offer no evidence that those killings were anything other than ordinary predation.

Conclusion

Seventeenth-century European villagers sought vampiric explanations during times of stress and fear, as did residents in many Latin American communities hundreds of years later. Puerto Rican society was also under unusual stress around the time that the chupacabra arrived on the island.

The island endured a long drought in the months and years leading up to the summer of 1995. There was also a looming hurricane, Marilyn, that was causing concern on the Caribbean island. In addition to the social stress and fear generated by an extended drought and looming hurricane, in 1994 and 1995 Puerto Rico endured an epidemic of dengue and dengue hemorrhagic fever (Rigau-Perez and Clark 2001). Nearly 25,000 people were struck down between June 1994 and May 1995; nearly 5,000 were hospitalized and 40 people died. This constituted the largest number of hospitalizations and deaths of any dengue epidemic in Puerto Rico's history. It is worth noting that the death and disease were spread by one of the deadliest known vampires: the bloodsucking mosquito (*Aedes aegypti*).

Pedro Vidal, a professor of Spanish and Latin American Studies at American University, notes that in the mid-1990s Puerto Rico was also in the grip of another disease that inspired worldwide fear and panic. The island was among the hardest hit by the AIDS epidemic at the time (Friedman 1996). It is of course difficult to pinpoint a specific cause of generalized fear and social anxiety, but there was clearly no shortage of things that concerned the Puerto Rican public around the time that *el chupacabra* was first sighted.

Lauren Derby offers an explanation for why the chupacabra might have begun specifically in the Canovanas area of Puerto Rico:

> One possible scenario is that the chupacabra initially emerged as a figure of Satan, a frightening changeling or shape shifter that provided a moralistic explanation for the run of small farm animal deaths that had plagued this interior mountainous region; these deaths may have been read as apocalyptic signs due to turn-of-the-millennium anxieties. Indeed, one of the first informants was Eliere Rivera, a Pentecostal priest, and mayor Chemo Soto, Margaret [*sic*] Tolentino, and her husband of course all form part of the tightly-knit Pentecostal community of Canovanas. Evangelical churches, with their strong interpersonal networks and media command have been found responsible for other rumors of remarkable spread such as the stories of Satanic ritual abuse that emerged around U.S. daycare centers in the late 1980s. (2008, 310)

Recall that in the case of the likichiri vampire of Chipaya, Bolivia, mentioned earlier, Pentecostal leaders were among the most fervent believers in (and persecutors of) the vampires.

Researcher Robert Jordan argues that the chupacabra as a symbol is "a form of cultural resistance which many people of Puerto Rico, Mexico, and the greater part of Latin America use to maintain social bonds and gain control over growing fears surrounding the perceived destructive effects of 'toxic' U.S. political and economic imperialism" (2008). Lauren Derby, writing in the journal *Past and Present*, argues that "the chupacabras belief was an urban legend, a popular commentary on modernity and its risks as they are perceived in Puerto Rico" (2008, 292). These may be valid cultural interpretations, and it is undoubtedly true that the chupacabra drew much of its notoriety and power from the fabric of Puerto Rican culture, society, and politics.

But these sociocultural explanations—valid as they may be—do little to silence the chupacabra believers and critics, who are impatient with such ivory tower, armchair speculations. Urban legends do not suck the blood out of thousands of goats, cattle, and chickens. Symbols of cultural resistance to American imperialism and exploitation are not seen by eyewitnesses with fearsome spikes down their spines as they bound over treetops. As one researcher asks, "Can the skeptic tell a distressed farmer that an 'archetype' or figment of the popular imagination just put a finger-sized hole through an animal's throat?" (Corrales 1997, 63). A fair question, and we can begin to answer it through an examination of how the chupacabra was seen in popular culture.

Chupacabras in Popular Culture

For a strange little Caribbean island creature that has never been photographed or even left any good evidence of its existence, the chupacabra has flourished as a global phenomenon. Though reported in only a dozen or so countries, the chupacabra is known and recognized worldwide. In this chapter I will first describe how the chupacabra was treated in the Puerto Rican press and on the streets, then turn to the chupacabra's many appearances in popular entertainment. A cycle was quickly established: animals thought to have been "mysteriously" killed by the chupacabra (or, far more rarely, a sighting of the creature) occurred, and were reported to the press. Those news reports, most of them alarmist and sensationalized, told hundreds of thousands (and eventually millions) of people about the chupacabra. The news reports in turn spawned more reports and sightings, and the process began anew, stronger than before. The chupacabra's meteoric rise in popularity was closely tied to the amount of publicity it received.

The Journalistic Chupacabra

In Puerto Rico, most of the initial chupacabra reports were spread through typical rumor routes: over back fences, among neighbors and friends: "Did you hear? Diego's cousin's friend had two goats sucked dry of blood last week! It must be *el chupacabra!*" But the creature's fame skyrocketed once local newspapers picked up the story and began publishing sensational headlines. Among the four newspapers that served Puerto Rico in 1995, *El Vocero* was among the most popular. It was "a tabloid whose headlines, in bright, red, uppercase letters, often surmount a grotesque photograph of a murder or automobile accident [with] consistent UFO/paranormal coverage" (Corrales 1997, 70). *El Vocero* was the *National Enquirer* of Puerto Rico, unashamedly promoting whatever lurid, shocking, or sensational story would help sell papers. And for Puerto Rico's favorite tabloid a mysterious animal-killing vampire was just the thing. No one was safe! Who would be next? Would it soon hunt humans? What *was* this strange beast? Elvis sightings and Bigfoot reports wouldn't stand a chance against the media's new bloodsucking menace.

This strong bias toward sensationalism affected the information that most Puerto Ricans got about the monster. Because the respectable, credible newspapers largely ignored the chupacabra stories, *El Vocero* happily filled the news void with its own dramatic brand of tabloid reporting. As a result, few Puerto Ricans who followed the mystery were exposed to the more level-headed, skeptical, and scientific analyses: panicked housewives and gun-toting farmers would always crowd out calm skeptics and scientists on newspaper pages.

Indeed, some people tried to calm fear by providing naturalistic explanations. Puerto Rican zoologist Edwin Velasquez noted during a radio interview that "[n]ot everyone can describe a creature they see at night, and their imagination fills in the blanks by association with other things. It happens very often in the Laguna Cartagena region, where feral monkeys escaped from a research institution. A person seeing one of these apes in twilight would believe they had seen a little man, thus confusing the real for the fantastic . . . This is dangerous, because when the humble, ignorant people of our rural areas hear there is a bloodsucking creature on the loose, they believe it. Hysteria sets in. We should not be so sensationalistic. The media, for whatever reason, only gives one part of the story rather than the whole story" (Corrales 1997, 27).

Myth, misinformation, rumor, and gossip were coin of the realm when it came to the chupacabra. In fact, the majority of chupacabra reports that circulated in Puerto Rico at the time were written by only a handful of *El Vocero* reporters; one in particular, Ruben Dario Rodriguez, accounted for nearly half of the stories. Rodriguez cranked out story after story, each more sensational than the last. Little wonder, then, that many of the chupacabra reports were similar—they were written by the same person.

The following must surely be the most outlandish chupacabra-related report (yet one that was reported as a straight news story, just as legitimate as the next): "Although five chickens were found entirely drained of blood in the back yard of the property owned by Julio and Julia Gonzales, the most spectacular event appears to have been the strange mark placed on the forearm of the couple's daughter . . . Oralis Gonzales, five years old, was marked with a tattoo-like impression that read, 'OJO-10-OJO' after an alleged encounter with non-human entities. While the child is reluctant to discuss exactly what transpired . . . it is generally acknowledged that this event has triggered the child's IQ, causing her father to describe her as a prodigy. Little Oralis's experience came to light while police officer Pablo Robles interviewed Mr. Gonzales about the dead poultry found in the back yard" (Corrales 1997, 78).

That's right: according to the eyewitnesses, the chupacabra abducted a five-year-old girl, then tattooed a series of letters and numbers on her forearm. It then escaped, and her experience with the chupacabra (or perhaps the tattoo) dramatically raised her intelligence to genius level. The story, which appeared in the November 13, 1995, issue of *El Vocero*, suggests that the incident was confirmed by a police officer, lending it some credibility. Despite this bizarre and astounding claim, nothing more is mentioned about the girl, her family, or the experience. Who tested little Oralis's genius IQ? What did doctors make of the supposed mysterious tattoo-like impressions? Though this is one of the more outlandish claims, in many ways it is typical of the chupacabra coverage. If this story—which is almost certainly a hoax—is treated with the same seriousness as all the other chupacabra stories, what credibility do any of them have? If *El Vocero* will pass off this self-evident chupadookie as true, what won't they print to sell a few papers? Because of stories like this, the credibility of many of the newspaper accounts (and therefore the "official" information about the Puerto Rican chupacabra) is highly suspect.

Leaping to Conclusions

With the chupacabra hysteria in full swing on the small island, any and all reports, no matter how outlandish, unlikely, or unverified, were widely reported and believed. People often jumped to illogical conclusions, attributing any odd event to the dreaded chupacabra. Take, for instance, the following report, from November 7, 1995: "Striking at a junkyard, it killed a cat and a sheep, and apparently swallowed an entire lamb, since the third animal being kept by the junkyard owner was never found." Exactly why the cat and sheep were assumed to have been chupacabra victims is not clear, but in the case of the lamb, there was no evidence at all that the chupacabra, or any other creature, had even encountered it. The lamb was not found dead, nor drained of blood; it was not found at all. It could have been stolen, or escaped from the yard, or any number of more likely explanations than assuming that the lamb must have obviously been swallowed whole by a chupacabra!

The Public's Reaction

The public reaction to the Puerto Rican chupacabra panic varied widely. One end of the spectrum included diehard UFO believers convinced that the sinister mystery likely had an extraterrestrial connection and was likely a very real threat to the island (if not the entire world). On the other end was the general public, who more or less ignored and gave little credence to stories of the bloodsucking beast, assuming it was either fictional, campy tabloid fodder (akin to *National Enquirer* reports of aliens and Bigfoot), or sincere but unfounded rumor spread by gullible *campesinos*—rural farmers and ranchers—seeking escapist entertainment. Most Puerto Ricans perhaps fell in between these extremes, not quite believing all the lurid stories, but suspecting that *something* strange might be out there.

Many Puerto Ricans saw the chupacabra as a *chiste* (joke), their very own local monster. This co-opting of monsters is actually quite common in areas where unknown or mysterious animals have been reported. In the state of Vermont, for example, the local lake monster Champ (which I extensively investigated in the book *Lake Monster Mysteries: Investigating the World's Most Elusive Creatures* [Radford and Nickell 2007]) has been adopted as a local mascot. Champ is depicted on T-shirts and souvenirs, on floats and parades, on signs, and so on. The minor league baseball team is even named after Champ: The Vermont Lake Monsters.

Canada's most famous lake monster, Ogopogo of Lake Okanagan, also exists as a regional hero and tourist attraction. Nicknamed Ogie, this public-friendly Ogopogo can be found peering down from shelves in tourist hovels, next to snow globes and plush beavers in little red Mounties uniforms. Ogopogo is devoid of scary scales or slimy skin, sheathed instead in a fuzzy and lovable countenance suitable for a beloved mascot. And, of course, Nessie of Scotland's Loch Ness long ago made the leap from monster to tourist attraction.

Scott Corrales (1997, 132) mentions several examples of chupacabra-inspired humor, including the suggestion of Puerto Rican political satirist Fernando Clemente that the first refugee from the 1996 Hurricane Hortense was none other than the chupacabra! Not only that, the jokester said, but San

Juan mayor José Soto had housed the creature in the city's town hall for its own protection, and would release it near election day to further his political career.

Some Puerto Ricans feared the chupacabra; others made fun of it, while many seized the opportunity to cash in on it. Tens of thousands of chupacabra-related T-shirts and apparel with many different designs were quickly marketed and sold. Chupacabra toys, books, and merchandise were manufactured. Several popular musicians wrote and recorded songs about the beast; one popular version contains the chorus "There's a buggy-eyed creature that they call the chupacabra / Four feet tall like a mutant winged Chihuahua / Mexico City, Puerto Rico, Nicaragua! / Hey chupacabra!"

It is common in writings about monsters for authors to exaggerate the degree and breadth of belief in (and fear surrounding) mysterious creatures. When reading accounts of the chupacabra in Puerto Rico, I often came across phrases like "the chupacabra terrorized the island" or "fear gripped Puerto Rico" or "the island populace was near fever pitch." There is of course some truth to this description, but mystery-mongering hyperbole aside, it is not accurate to suggest that the entire Puerto Rican population—or even a majority of it—was gripped in terror over the goatsucker. Of course some individuals and groups grew very concerned over the mystery, but most Puerto Ricans (especially city dwellers) went about their daily lives giving little thought or concern to the creature they had heard about mostly in backyard gossip and tabloids.[1]

This is not to say that panic and hysteria over the chupacabra did not sweep over some parts of the island in 1995, for they surely did. Concerned citizens formed patrols and vigilante mobs hoping to find the chupacabra. Ranchers brought rifles, farmers bore pitchforks, while ordinary citizens made do with baseball bats and sticks. In one case the death of forty sheep at a ranch near the town of Los Mochis-Topolobambo prompted "a massive mobilization of searchers outfitted with infrared lights, shotguns, electrical equipment, helmets, and riot shields" (Corrales 1996, 142). Furthermore, local authorities "led 200-strong search parties on nightly forays" to capture the chupacabra. Despite such a sustained, coordinated effort, no trace of the beast was found.

Despite the fear and concern, there was very little actual investigation into what, exactly, was going on. Amateur paranormal investigators and groups (mostly UFO buffs) took it upon themselves to look into some of the sightings; while their sincerity is not in question (they certainly believed they were doing good research), their methods were usually far from thorough or scientific and followed no discernible investigative strategy. Sightings were more often than not simply *recorded* rather than *investigated*; eyewitnesses who could have supported (or refuted) the main eyewitness accounts were rarely interviewed; there was little systemic collection of evidence, and so on.

Investigation

Because chupacabra reports were not criminal matters, police, government officials, and trained investigators rarely got involved. The notable exception was the mayor of San Juan, José "Chemo" Soto, who formed a group of "Rambos, the militia-like posse of fearless goatsucker hunters," to search for the chupacabra. Soto's involvement with the chupacabra has been questioned by some who suggest that his well-publicized search for the creatures was little more than a political publicity stunt allowing him to be seen as a macho fearless leader willing to do battle with an unknown, vampiric killer on behalf of his terror-ridden city and its voters. The gregarious and photogenic Soto (nicknamed "Chemo Jones" after the adventure-seeking hero Indiana Jones) was always happy to use the goatsucker as an excuse to get in front of a television camera.

There are a handful of accounts of police investigations of chupacabra reports, but with only bizarre, contradictory descriptions and stories there was little the police could do. This of course frustrated a frightened public who demanded protection from the vampire beast lurking in the shadows.

The Pop Culture Chupacabra

For as much fear and concern as the chupacabra generated (at least initially among Puerto Ricans), the goatsucker was almost as enthusiastically embraced by the wider Hispanic and Spanish-speaking communities; this juxtaposition reveals, in part, a divide between social classes: while famous musicians, comics, entertainers, and urban literati treated the beast as a fanciful myth like Bigfoot or furry Dracula, it was no joke in the rural areas among hard-working farmers and blue-collar workers. The chupacabra was not a threat to urban professionals such as dentists and businessmen; it was a threat to the working class, those whose livestock might be vulnerable to the beast. Whether the chupacabra was real or not, it at least had the potential to be a threat.

In addition to music and songs about the chupacabra that arose in Puerto Rico in 1996, many other artists released songs in its wake. For example, pop singer Imani Coppola's 1997 debut album was named *Chupacabra*; one band called Soil had a 1998 EP album called *El Chupacabra!* (featuring silhouettes of a chupacabra menacing a nude woman); and a Colorado-based World Funk band called Chupacabra took its name "in reference to the yearning of the human spirit to be connected with something greater" (whatever that means).

Chupacabra Films

Like other cryptids such as Bigfoot and the Loch Ness monster, the chupacabra has been the subject of several mainstream films. Most of them are grade-B splatter films such as *El Chupacabra* (2003), whose plot is described as follows on the DVD jacket copy: "After being captured in the wilderness, the murderous monster of Mexican legend—known as El Chupacabra—escapes into the city and begins a murderous spree. A scientist and an animal control officer set out to capture the beast and soon realize that a ruthless vigilante has been hired by the villainous Dr. Goodspeed to catch the monster for his own purposes." A step or two above is *Chupacabra Terror* (2005), starring John Rhys-Davies (of *Indiana Jones and the Temple of Doom* fame) and Giancarlo Esposito as "a cryptozoologist who has dedicated his life to studying the mysterious and elusive mythical monster, the chupacabra. When he finally manages to capture one on a remote Caribbean island, he stands to become a legend himself within the scientific community—that is, if he can manage to get the beast back to the U.S. He smuggles it on board a cruise ship, but it's not long before curiosity gets the better of a couple of porters, who open the crate to see what's inside; the released creature proceeds to go on a rampage, turning the ship into an enormous bloodbath." (All film synopses are from the Internet Movie Database, IMDb.com.)

Along similar lines is *Bloodthirst: Legend of the Chupacabra* (2003). The film's theme seems to include elements of leprechaun legend: "When a strange map turns up in a small, isolated town, the citizens believe it will lead them to a long-lost mysterious treasure. Dreaming of riches, they follow the trail into the hills where they find an unspeakable terror and death. It is a path leading them to the lair of a deadly killer, the mythic chupacabra and not the pot of gold they expected." Apparently the film left some unresolved issues, because three years later a sequel was released: *Bloodthirst 2: Revenge of the Chupacabras*. A 2007 film titled *Legend of the Chupacabra* (fortunately for the

Figure 5. Video cover for *Chupacabra Terror* (2004), one of many horror films starring the bloodthirsty Hispanic vampire beast.

filmmakers, titles of books and films cannot be copyrighted) is slightly closer to a realistic depiction of actual chupacabra reports: "A mysterious creature kills a herd of goats and the man who owns them, and is seen committing the devious deed on videotape. A family member cuts her bereavement short and rounds up some villagers to hunt the killer down, with predictably bloody results." Not to be outdone, a 2007 film called *Mexican Werewolf in Texas* (a clumsy reference to the 1981 John Landis film *An American Werewolf in London*) tells the story of teens in a small Texas town plagued by mysterious killings that, of course, turn out to be the work of the chupacabra.

For the more genteel chupacabra aficionados who prefer comedy and nudity to gore, there's the 2006 Spanish-language *Ataca El Chupacabra* (Attack of the chupacabra) about an alcoholic who gets bitten by a chupacabra, and "develops a taste for blood himself. Searching the streets night after night, he feeds only on the sexiest women in sight." Those horny, wacky chupacabras also appeared in another Spanish-language film released in 2007, *Ahi Viene El Chupacabras* (Here comes the chupacabras), in which "an alien used to feeding on animal blood turns its attention to human virgins when it crash lands on Earth." Hide your virgins! (and, apparently, your cows).

It is interesting to note that the only films that treat the chupacabra as a joke or source of comedy are those from the creature's supposed homeland: Latin America. North American films treat the chupacabra as a genuine threat and object of fear and horror, while Spanish-language films treat it as an object of mocking and humor. It seems that, as with the chupacabra in a larger context, it is mostly foreigners—not locals—who take the creature seriously.

The chupacabra was also the subject of a popular *X-Files* episode ("El Mundo Gira," season 4, episode 11) in which Mulder and Scully investigate the death of a young migrant worker. Given the production schedule for the television show (the episode aired January 12, 1997), the writer likely began working on the story in early 1996, just as the chupacabra scare was waning in Puerto Rico but spreading to Mexico, Nicaragua, and other countries.

Chupacabra in Literature

The chupacabra as a literary entity didn't appear until about 2005. For the first decade after the 1995 Puerto Rican sightings, it was folklore in the making, as the idea of the Latin American vampiric goatsucker percolated. Perhaps some writers were reluctant to write much about the creature as fiction, believing that the chupacabra might be found—and its existence proven—at any time. Others may have waited to see how the chupacabra story would unfold, what forms it would take around the world.

Whatever the reason, the chupacabra that eventually emerged in literature was a very different animal than the 1995 Puerto Rican bloodthirsty beast. In fact, the vast majority of goatsucker appearances are in children's books.

One of the most famous writers to use the beast in fiction is Rudolfo Anaya, a venerated founder of modern Chicano literature. Anaya, a native New Mexican, wrote a 2006 children's book titled *Curse of the ChupaCabra*. Aimed at young adults, the story follows a university professor named Rose Medina whose interest in chupacabra folklore leads her to Mexico to investigate a man's death blamed on the goatsucker. There she discovers that the chupacabra is being used by drug runners trafficking in methamphetamines.

Medina sets out to stop the chupacabra before it can kill again, while fighting the scourge of drugs invading America's youth (Anaya 2006).

Anaya revisited the chupacabra two years later in his book *ChupaCabra and the Roswell UFO* (Anaya 2008), also published by the University of New Mexico Press, in which Medina narrowly escapes a nighttime chupacabra attack and travels to Roswell to stop an evil scientist from doing genetics experiments involving extraterrestrial aliens and chupacabras. This plot has echoes of the science fiction film *Species* (see chapter 7).

Another children's book, a storybook from 2006 for kids ages four to eight, is *Juan and the Chupacabras*, by Xavier Garza. The thirty-two-page story (presented in both English and Spanish) involves a pair of young cousins who wonder if their grandfather's tall tales of battling chupacabra are real or not. Still another children's chupacabra tome is a 2007 book called *Chupacabra*, by Terry O'Neill, written for ages nine to twelve. *Night of the Chupacabras*, by Marie G. Lee and published in 1999, is also written for ages nine to twelve. Like *Juan and the Chupacabras*, it is a multilingual story (English, Spanish, and Korean), and features a young Korean girl named Mi-Sun who hears old-timer stories about the chupacabra and decides to find out for herself if they are true or not. Other children's books about the chupacabra include *El Chupacabras: Trail of the Goatsucker*, by Lloyd Wagner (2004), and *The Fairy and the Chupacabra and Those Marfa Lights*, by James A. Mangum and Sidney Spires (2008).

In all, there are nearly a dozen books that involve the chupacabra creature, most of them written for young children. The chupacabras that appear in these books have of course been sanitized; there are no references to cow-raping, slime-spewing, gory carcasses, or real danger to children. Most treat the chupacabra as mere myth, a wink-and-nod creature only a step or two removed from unicorns or dragons. In the comic book world, a special edition of the Marvel title *The Fantastic Four* featured the chupacabra in 2007 (fig. 6). The story, titled "Isla de la Muerte" (Island of death) was set in Puerto Rico and revealed the goatsucker to be a beast under the control of the Fantastic Four's old nemesis the Mole Man.

An interesting folkloric take on the chupacabra legend can be found in the book *Caribbean Mythology and Modern Life: Five One-Act Plays for Young People*, by Paloma Mohamed (2003). The first play in the book, "Chupacabra," deals with HIV/AIDS in the context of Caribbean culture, and draws its characters from various Latin American mythologies (for example, the Ole Higue—a variation of the Old Hag/succubus archetype—of Guyana folklore,

Figure 6. Spanish-language version of Marvel Comics' *Fantastic Four*, in which the superheroes battle the chupacabra.

and the bloodsucker Obayifo from African myths; see Hufford 1982). One reviewer, Tanya Batson-Savage of Jamaica's *Sunday Gleaner*, commended "the interesting use of mythology provides an innovative take on the HIV/AIDS epidemic. However, while the play creates a good platform for building awareness about the disease, it does not explore the issue sufficiently. As such, the play tackles issues such as the need for abstinence and the rampant spread of the disease. . . . Unfortunately, as with many productions which attempt to tackle the AIDS issue, 'Chupacabra' is disappointing in the end, forgetting the magical power it wields and falling to preaching instruction instead" (Batson-Savage 2006). The link between vampires and AIDS has been explored before in fiction, and a UFO cult called NOVA claimed in 1995 that the chupacabra was in fact an extraterrestrial alien trying to infect humans with diseases such as AIDS—though adding the chupacabra in a didactic children's play about AIDS is an interesting twist.

The Sideshow Goatsucker

Outside of fiction, there is one other place in popular culture where the goatsucker can be found: it can be seen for a dollar or two at state fairs and in sideshows. Bizarre curiosities (both real and "gaffed") have always been staples of the sideshows, and the chupacabra is a natural. One sideshow banner on a midway at the 2005 Erie County (New York) Fair shows a green-skinned, fanged and clawed chupacabra pouncing on a goat (fig. 7); below that is an image of the feared Mongolian Death Worm, and passersby may suppose the pair are just inside the tent, caged but otherwise ready to eviscerate and exsanguinate any unwary onlooker. Another banner depicts a gargoyle-like winged chupacabra about to take a bite out of a terrified goat.

Figure 7. Sideshow banner at the 2005 Erie County Fair advertising a chupacabra. Photo by the author.

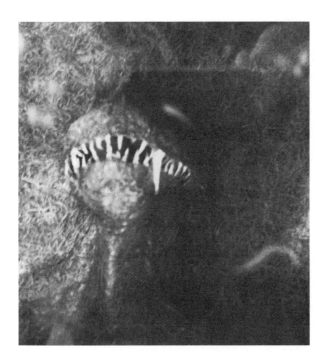

Figure 8. A dead "chupacabra" displayed at a sideshow at the 2009 New Mexico State Fair. Photo by the author.

The banners are of course sensationalized, but what is the nature of the beast lurking inside? A sideshow exhibit by the famous showman Bobby Reynolds at the 2009 New Mexico State Fair contained a short, dark human-oid creature with a gaping maw of sharp teeth (fig. 8). Of course, it was no more or less real than any of the other exhibits, but surely worth two dollars of entertainment value. Ironically, the exhibit also contained a second animal that had been claimed as the chupacabra yet clearly was not, a faked creature called a Jenny Haniver (see "A Chupacabra Named Jenny" in chapter 5).

The inclusion of the chupacabra in the sideshows tells us something about its semimythical status in American culture. After all, the exhibits contained no alleged Bigfoot bodies or Loch Ness fins; perhaps the top two mysterious creatures in the world were not deemed to be taken seriously enough by the public to bother including. The chupacabra's relatively low profile (compared to its more famous cousins) and legions of people who genuinely believe in its existence may have helped it earn a seat at the carnival table. (Much in the same way that many musicians feel they have "made it" when their song is parodied by satirist Weird Al Yankovic, the chupacabra seems to have "made it" when its doppelganger fake is displayed.)

Figure 9. A "mummified chupacabra fetus" gaffe sold on eBay. Photo by the author.

Online auctions such as those on eBay occasionally offer chupacabra-related items, from T-shirts to figurines to comic books. In 2009 the company Topps/Allen and Ginter issued a trading card series titled "Creatures of Legend, Myth, and Terror," which included the chupacabra as one of the star monsters depicted (along with the unicorn, Loch Ness monster, minotaur, and other creatures). A search of chupacabra-related items for sale on eBay gives some measure of the animal's popularity. One enterprising individual even offered chupacabra repellent for $15 per bottle in an August 2008 listing. The item description stated, "I have been using our homemade chupacabra repellent for 23 years and haven't had any chupacabra problems yet. It is the best on the market and is 100% effective, and works on pets too . . . Also effective on uni-cabras, hezbocabras, etc . . . basically effective anything in the cabra family." Others offer all manner of T-shirts, stuffed toys, and other novelties. In 2008 a card game called Chupacabra was published by Café Games.

The game allows players to pretend they are the creature. You can even purchase a custom-made "chupacabra fetus" online (fig. 9).

The Christian Chupacabra

El chupacabra's cultural influence includes religious belief, and many who believe in the beast think that it must have some important divine purpose. For those Christians wondering, "So how does this Hispanic goatsucking chupacabra thing fit in with God's plan?," a man named James Lloyd has the answer. Lloyd, founder of the Christian Media Network ministry, wrote a book titled *Chupacabras: The Devil's Genetics*, in which he explains how Bible prophecy predicted the arrival of the chupacabra, which in turn would signal the start of Armageddon (fig. 10). He links the chupacabra with the hideous monsters mentioned in Revelations 9: "The locusts looked like

Figure 10. *Chupacabras: The Devil's Genetics*, a booklet by James Lloyd of the Christian Media Network.

horses prepared for battle. On their heads they wore something like crowns of gold, and their faces resembled human faces. Their hair was like women's hair, and their teeth were like lions' teeth. They had breastplates like breastplates of iron, and the sound of their wings was like the thundering of many horses and chariots rushing into battle. They had tails and stings like scorpions, and in their tails they had power to torment people for five months." The chupacabra, Lloyd believes, was created through genetic engineering as a weapon, and will attack humanity alongside demons collectively named Legion (from the Gospel of Mark 5:9).

"When you strip away the sensational aspects of this enigma, the fact remains that reputable and credible witnesses have seen and identified the chupacabra as the predator that has killed quite a few animals" (Lloyd 2001). Lloyd subscribes to the popular belief that the goatsucker may have been created in an experiment, engineered to prey on Puerto Ricans: "Technically speaking, the creation of something like the chupacabra does not pose a particularly difficult scientific challenge. . . . With what we already know about unrestrained intelligence agency driven research, to suspect that military or intelligence groups are field testing a transgenic specie/weapon on remote populations is not that hard to believe. Indeed, evidence that such creatures exist is found in the Bible. The book Revelation describes creatures that are scheduled to be unleashed, apparently as genetic weapons, during the tribulation" (Lloyd 2001, 17). According to Lloyd, the chupacabra would be the perfect weapon in the hands of the great Satanic powers: "Such creatures would be devastating in a military conflict. They would attack people, but leave the environment alone. The black science that created them probably includes the equivalent of an 'on/off' switch so they could be disabled at the conclusion of their usefulness."

Lloyd is not alone in his beliefs. Rev. Francisco Ortiz, head of a Pentecostal church in Nicaragua, stated that he also believed the chupacabra to be a sign that the End Times were near. Ortiz told his followers that it was "a warning sign . . . a sign for men and women to return to God because we've forgotten about him" (quoted in Greste 2000). Ortiz cited Bible scripture (particularly the Book of Daniel) to prove his case. Picking up on the notion that the chupacabra is the unholy result of strange science experiments, Reverend Ortiz took the opportunity to rail against genetic manipulation and cloning as human evil that "contradicts God's mandate."

Another fundamentalist Christian, John Adolfi, purchased an alleged chupacabra (found in Blanco, Texas; see chapter 5) and displayed it in his creationist museum as an example of the fallibility of science. Adolfi's Lost World Museum (named after Sir Arthur Conan Doyle's 1912 novel in which dinosaurs still exist) features items and artifacts that he believes prove that scientists don't have all the answers. A creationist, Adolfi believes that Earth was created six thousand to ten thousand years ago by God, and that the world's scientists are wrong about the age of the Earth. He believes that by displaying the chupacabra, he casts doubt on the credibility of mainstream scientists (Lundborg 2009). If scientists scoff at the chupacabra's existence (yet here it obviously is!), could they also be wrong about evolution and the age of Earth? In 2010 Adolfi loaned his science-busting chupacabra to another religious museum in Crosbyton, Texas, called The Mt. Blanco Fossil Museum and Independent Creationist Association. Other Christians, espousing per-haps less extreme views, reject the idea that the chupacabra is a genetically engineered weapon, but nonetheless believe it represents diabolical forces.

From its roots as a vampire to its role as an agent of Armageddon and symbol of American imperialism, the chupacabra has a rich history. If the chupacabra were depicted in a painting, these would be the vivid details that set the stage and create the background. Yet the monster in the foreground is obscure. Its form is suggested and hinted at, but the beast itself, the focus of the piece, remains frustratingly shadowy. We have the background, the social and cultural world in which the chupacabra exists. We must now fill in the foreground.

PART III

SEARCH FOR THE CHUPACABRA

4

Searching for
Chupacabras in Nicaragua

I n the years I spent researching the chupacabra I kept coming back to the fundamental question: Is the chupacabra real? I didn't have the answer, but I was willing to make a real effort to find out. It's relatively easy to sit in an armchair and issue learned (and not-so-learned) speculations, but it's quite another to head into the jungle in search of the vampire beast. There is a rich history—even in modern times—of launching expeditions to find unknown, possibly mythical creatures. The subjects are not dragons, mermaids, unicorns, or other creatures of lore, but so-called monsters. Often the searches are begun with great enthusiasm, fanfare, and hoopla, but almost invariably end with a whimper and little if any evidence (what there is of it ambiguous). In 1873 showman P. T. Barnum offered huge cash rewards for the capture of Champ, the lake monster said to inhabit Lake Champlain; the bounty sent amateur expeditions tumbling over each other in fruitless searches of the lake (Radford and Nickell 2007).

More recently, researcher Robert Rines spent decades searching Loch Ness for its mysterious denizen, without definitive results. Oilman Tom Slick, along with Rene Dahinden, Ivan Sanderson, and many others, searched in vain for Bigfoot (see McLeod 2009 for a fuller account), and there have been dozens of searches (with wildly varying degrees of professionalism) to find the Yeti (formerly known as the Abominable Snowman), the dinosaur-like Mokele-Mbembe in central Africa, and so on. I, both independently and with colleague Joe Nickell, launched many expeditions over the past decade searching for Bigfoot and lake monsters (see our book *Lake Monster Mysteries: Investigating the World's Most Elusive Creatures*, 2007).

In 2009, with this robust history of gumption (and near-spotless track record of failure) in mind, I decided to launch an expedition into the jungles of Nicaragua in search of the chupacabra. Of all the Latin American countries, Nicaragua boasts one of the most famous and intriguing chupacabra sightings on record (see chapter 5). The more I researched Nicaragua, the more likely it seemed that chupacabras might exist there. If a famous 2000 sighting was authentic—and chupacabras did indeed existed in Nicaragua—why have the sightings tapered off? Perhaps a farmer shot the last surviving chupacabra in that country, but more likely the creatures simply migrated to more hospitable areas. Wild animals across the globe have lost precious habitat to humans, whether through building, farming, logging, or ranching. Chupacabras would need room to roam, a ready supply of prey, and a place where they could exist undetected. There is one ideal place in Nicaragua where the chupacabra would thrive: the jungles of the Indio Maiz Biological Reserve near the Rio San Juan, along the southern border with Costa Rica. The area covers about 2,800 square miles and is home to more species of trees, birds, and insects than exist in all of Europe.

Though little mentioned today, for many years the Rio San Juan held strategic international importance as a link between the Atlantic and Pacific oceans. In fact, during the nineteenth century the river was the fastest route between New York and San Francisco. After Panama's more favorable topography allowed that country's canal to be constructed in the early twentieth century, international and political interest in the area faded (Power 2006). Over the centuries, the Rio San Juan carried pirates of many nationalities, as well as African slaves, dignitaries, famous military heroes, and even a young writer named Mark Twain in 1866, who described the area as "an earthy paradise." Yet it was a paradise limned with death: many of his fellow passengers died in a cholera outbreak aboard their steamship. Though Twain escaped infection, later in his voyage he described the diseased dead being brought to the ship's deck covered in sheets and dumped overboard to feed the waiting sharks.

The area is remote and difficult to get to, and access to the Bioreserve is strictly controlled and patrolled. Visitors must obtain a permit and be accompanied by an official park guide while in the area. Hunting and logging are forbidden, and only guides may stay there. Because of such restrictions, animals are plentiful (including puma, jaguar, boar, tapir, and monkeys). Chupacabras would be able to prey on native animals more or less unnoticed.

There is another good reason to think that the chupacabras, if they exist, might lurk under the jungle canopy. If the creatures originally came from the jungles of Puerto Rico, as is widely believed, it seems likely that they would find the jungle habitat much more hospitable than the open, high and dry desert areas in central and northern Nicaragua.

A few previous chupacabra expeditions had been conducted, with varying degrees of academic rigor and uniformly negative results. In 1998, Jon Downes made a trip to Puerto Rico to search for the beast, returning to the island six years later with his colleague Nick Redfern for a television show (2001). To the best of my knowledge, this was the first full expedition in Central America.

The persistent, rhythmic watch alarm roused me from a restless sleep. The room was dark; in the night I had sensed some creature above or around me. I had visions of some strange, feral entity lurking nearby. Whatever its nature—animal, hallucination, or some mad combination of both—it was gone. Through the gauzy mosquito net and the open-air window I could see the first inklings of a sunrise outlined above the ragged silhouette of jungle canopy. In the inky distance I heard a chorus of deep guttural growls and howls from the treetops. I sighed, partly cursing the young hour and partly relieved to end the night. I sorely wanted to remain in bed, but I roused myself anyway.

For the Nicaragua chupacabra expedition, I was joined by colleague Chris Ayles and my father, Jeff, himself a veteran of Latin American travel. The plan was to spend five days in the jungle searching for animals including the chupacabra. We would fly to the capital city of Managua, then head south to the town of San Carlos on the southeastern shore of Lake Nicaragua where the Rio San Juan begins its nearly 125 mile journey to the Caribbean. From there we'd hire a boat downriver to the village of El Castillo, and finally to a tiny lodge near the Bartola River.

As it turned out, simply getting to the Rio San Juan was an adventure by itself. I will spare readers the tedious details of typical Latin American travel delays, but the first problem we encountered was that only one local airline serviced San Carlos. Because of the paucity of flights and the tiny planes, the next two days of departures were full. We had already gathered expedition supplies in Managua, and rather than spend idle time there, we booked passage on a bus headed south the next morning.

We arrived by taxi at a cavernous, concrete bus station, just beginning to crawl with vendors and travelers in the cool morning air. Our bus was not one of the comfortable *ejecutivo* buses that ply Central American highways on long routes, with reclining seats and window shades. Instead, we were loaded onto a vintage American school bus that, judging from its state of decrepitude, had been retired in the 1970s at the age in which only prayer and constant repair would keep it mobile. We left just before dawn for a twelve-hour trip, the final third of which was on unpaved, rutted, bone-rattling roads. It was a true "chicken bus"—the slender, middle-aged man in the seat ahead of me next to Chris had two fowl with him, one in a small duffel bag at his feet and the second one in his lap. The bagged chicken was docile, any nervous energy likely drained by the bag's darkness, while the one in his lap grew agitated every twenty minutes, fluttering and clucking. The man held it tight, careful not to choke it.

We finally arrived at the tiny, dusty port of San Carlos. We searched for our lodgings, then made arrangements to be taken farther downriver to El Castillo, home of an impressive fort (or castle, *castillo*) built around 1675 by the Spanish. Overlooking an area of treacherous white water called The Devil's Rapids (*Raudal El Diablo*), the fortress fended off pirates for centuries. British Vice-Admiral Horatio Nelson succeeded in taking the fort in 1780, though the victory (like his soldiers) was short-lived; he soon abandoned the fort when malaria felled his soldiers by the score. A few enterprising people had tried to take over the whole country at one point or another, yet all the lawyers, guns, and money in the world couldn't make the regimes last.

As far as we'd come by plane, bus, and boat, we were still some distance from our final destination yet farther downriver. The travel delays cost about two days of time scheduled for the expedition, but nothing could be done about it. As we travelled farther from Managua, the towns grew smaller and the accommodations grew sparser. Few dwellings had air conditioning; instead floor fans provided some relief from the heat—when electricity was available. Even local communication was spotty, with news and messages often relayed through travelers and commuters between river towns; even cell phones worked only as often as not. At a location this remote, medical emergencies were a concern; the nearest hospital was at least a day away, and serious accident or attack victims could easily bleed to death waiting for medical help.

As we journeyed downriver, I was surprised to see livestock grazing in patches along the northern shore. In Spanish, I asked our guide about it, and he said that there are many cattle ranches along the Rio San Juan; in fact ranching was the main industry in the area. I realized that ranches would provide a large and continuous supply of cattle for any chupacabras to feed

Figure 11. The San Juan River in the jungles of Nicaragua, Central America, one of the most likely places to find an existing population of chupacabras. Photo by the author.

upon. They would have no need to scavenge or raid rural ranches for food; they could prey at will. If chupacabras exist, the jungle along the San Juan was an ideal place, not only in Nicaragua but perhaps in all of Central America, for them to thrive.

Day 1: Arrival

We arrived at our destination in late afternoon by canoe to find a series of thatched huts in a clearing between the jungle and two rivers. There were no telephones. Limited electricity was provided by a generator, and cold, not-completely-dirty water dripped from the shower. The windows contained no glass (merely wooden shutters that deterred none but the laziest of insects) and suspended mosquito nets cascaded around the beds. There were three empty rooms, and we were the only guests. A glance through the lodge's rain-spot-pocked guestbook revealed only a few dozen visitors had stayed there in the previous six months.

The staff of two (one cook/housekeeper and her assistant) introduced us to Fernando Casanova, a local wildlife expert and official Indio Maiz Biological Reserve park guide. During our brief meeting he agreed to take us out early the next morning in search of animals. I was thinking nine o'clock would be adequate, but he convinced us that our best chance for spotting any animals was earlier—much earlier. I masked my annoyance with an agreeable smile and set my watch alarm for 5:30.

We unloaded our packs, donned hiking gear, and ventured into the rainforest for one hike before dark. The jungle, as seen on film and television in the cool comfort of a movie theater or living room couch, is close to Twain's "earthy paradise." Brightly colored birds squawk, insects busily build or destroy, and monkeys chase each other over treetop islands.

Yet real dangers lurk amid the verdant curtains. The jungle teems with both large, carnivorous predators and microscopic, opportunistic bacteria. Even minor wounds that might merely merit a Band-Aid in less remote places must be regarded with care, lest they become infected. Jungles are home to more forms of death and disease than any other environment on earth.

A sense of the surreal permeates the jungle. This is a place of constant movement and rhythmic sounds—clicking, whirring, croaking, and bird calls of all meter and description. There is activity on all sides, directly above and below the feet—much of it obscured by dense foliage, thick trees, and steep hills. Trees climb impossible heights in search of sunlight, and plants develop leaves as large as windshields to snatch what little light trickles down through the canopy. This is a place where tree sap can cure disease and ants can kill. Some local lore even holds that certain trees can walk across the forest floor (Radford 2009). As I tried to sleep in the sticky night air I realized that in this world the idea of chupacabras lurking amid the giant leaves can seem credible.

Day 2: The Search Begins

The next morning, after very grudgingly arising from bed, we collected our gear: flashlights, cameras, containers for collecting samples, and so on. Fernando met us near our hut and we headed out. As we hiked the dark trails we often heard animals before we saw them. Fernando led us a mile or so, and for an hour we tracked families of howler monkeys and spider monkeys high above us, watching them swing effortlessly from tree to tree.

We found that the jungle environment presents its own set of unique difficulties for spotting animals. For one thing, in our everyday lives we are

Figure 12. Indio Maiz Biological Reserve officer Fernando Casanova guides the author and his colleagues through Nicaragua's jungle in search of the chupacabra. Photo by Chris Ayles.

accustomed to mostly focusing our attention at eye level or below: cars, doors, desks, passersby on the street, and so on. Often what is directly above us (ceilings) and below us (floors) is ignored as both obvious and predictable.

Yet the jungle is a 360-degree experience. No matter which direction you look, animals can be (and often are) above, behind, around, and below you. Visitors who spend their time looking up and around will discover many hidden animals, though paying such attention can come at a dear price. Those looking up at the trees are not looking down at the trail, which is constantly cluttered with ankle-wrenching vines, roots, and branches. Pausing still and silent is the most effective way to locate animals, though even staying motionless invites hazards. It gives hungry mosquitoes a chance to swarm around any exposed skin, and if you're not careful you may unwittingly pause while standing on top of one of the many nearly invisible ant trails that crisscross the jungle floor, bearing a caravan of ants carrying tiny leaf fragments. While you are gazing into the dark canopy above and around, you may not notice the dozens of ants silently climbing your boots and pants (as I discovered from personal experience).

We trooped on, taking in the jungle greenery, but didn't see any sign of chupacabras. That afternoon after returning to camp I interviewed Fernando about the goatsucker and any other mysterious animals that might lurk in the area. As it turned out, he had begun his career as a guide in 2001—just after the most famous chupacabra sighting in Nicaragua (see next chapter).

Figure 13. The author discusses chupacabra sightings and tracks with guide Fernando Casanova of Nicaragua's Indio Maiz Biological Reserve. Photo by Jeff Radford.

"What is your understanding of the chupacabra's character or description?" I asked.

"Well, of course it sucks blood," he replied in Spanish. "It has big ears, a snout like a coyote or a dog. It has hairy legs, and fur on its back and torso."

I asked Fernando if he believed the chupacabra existed. He smiled and shook his head. "No, I do not think it is a real animal. We have strange animals here, but not that."

I realized that, despite Fernando's extensive knowledge of the jungle flora and fauna, he might not be as likely to encounter the chupacabra as would a nearby rancher whose livelihood depended on raising some of the creature's favorite prey.

"What about the farmers and ranchers who live around here, along the San Juan? Do they believe in the chupacabra?"

Fernando laughed. "No. They are more afraid of mad cow disease or jaguars than of chupacabra," he said.

"Have you heard of any reports of cattle being attacked by anything mysterious, or drained of blood?" I asked.

"Of course, it happens that sometimes cattle are attacked, but nothing like that. Nothing drained of blood or mysterious. [The chupacabra] is a thing that is never seen, only heard of—something other people see or tell stories about."

I later spoke to several locals in El Castillo, but could find no reports of any mysterious livestock predation. If chupacabras live in the area, they seem to have given up their famous thirst for livestock blood in favor of more exotic prey.

That evening, after a dinner of fish and rice, we headed to our rooms before the mosquitoes turned out in force. The electric generator was turned off nightly about an hour after sunset to conserve fuel. To save flashlight batteries we lit some stubby white candles we found on a shelf in our room as we prepared for bed. The window shutters were open to catch the river's breeze, and each separate dying candle wrought its ghost upon the wooden floor, dancing as the flame tossed to and fro, popping softly as gnats and moths succumbed to its beguiling glow.

Late that night in the darkness I thought I heard something moving above me. While I nodded, nearly napping, suddenly there came a tapping, as of something gently flapping above our wooden door. A faint whooshing sound, difficult to distinguish from the screeching cicadas, croaking frogs, and chirping crickets. I flicked on my trusty Maglight and played it around the hut, but didn't see anything. Chris asked what I saw or heard, confiding that he, too, had slept fitfully, unnerved by his own vivid experiences. Instead of replacing my flashlight on the floor, I kept it at the ready under my pillow. I remembered that some eyewitnesses claim the chupacabra has wings. My rational mind didn't really think that we were being stalked or watched by the chupacabra—or anything else for that matter—but my irrational and subconscious mind eagerly entertained my phantom fears. A tired mind can become a shape-shifter.

Day 3: Tracking the Chupacabra

In light of our continuing and collective lack of sleep, I refused to begin our second morning any earlier than necessary, though I was up by about seven o'clock anyway. We fell into a familiar pattern: once again we began with a hike, this time taking a new trail. We returned for breakfast within a few hours, rested, and headed out again, then returned for a late lunch.

After eating I wanted to go for a longer hike, but it was too hot to venture out again. The midday sun was scorching, and even the quarter-mile walk to the farthest trailhead seemed more than we could muster. Finally, after a few hours of rest in shaded hammocks we explored a different trail. Wanting to get further afield (and seeking a respite from the heat), we took a canoe trip partway up the Bartola River to a lagoon, leaving the heat to mad dogs and Englishmen.

Our hikes and searches had not yielded any sightings, but I had prepared another strategy. No matter how shy or well hidden any chupacabras might be, there was one piece of evidence that would be impossible to hide: their tracks.

One of the biggest difficulties in trying to find unknown creatures (such as Bigfoot, lake monsters, or chupacabras) is the lack of any valid references. For example, we know what a bear track looks like; if we find a track that we *suspect* was left by a bear, we can compare it to one we *know* was left by a bear. But there are no undisputed Bigfoot or chupacabra specimens by which to compare new evidence. Newly discovered tracks that don't look like older samples are generally not taken as proof that one (or both) sets are fakes, but instead that the new tracks are simply from a different animal, or from a different species or family. What we have, then, are new tracks, hairs, and other evidence being compared to *known* hoaxed tracks, hairs, etc. as well as *possibly* hoaxed tracks, hair, etc.

There are, however, a few reputed chupacabra casts and tracks claimed by one expert or another as valid evidence. Though these myriad tracks may or may not have actually been made by a chupacabra, until we have a scientifically validated track, they are among the best we have. The first specimen was presented at the 2006 *Fortean Times* UnConvention, courtesy of Jon Downes. It is identical to a chupacabra track in the collection of Virgilio Sanchez-Ocejo of the Miami UFO Center—the authenticity of which Downes and others have disputed (see chapter 1).

The second track is from a photograph of an alleged chupacabra foot owned by curio collector Johnny Fox in his New York City–based museum The Freakatorium: El Museo Loco (fig. 14). While the museum houses some

Figure 14. An alleged chupacabra foot, from the collection of magician and raconteur Johnny Fox in his now-defunct El Museo Loco in New York City. Photo by the author.

gaffes (faked items, in carnival slang), it also contains many indisputably authentic items of cryptozoological interest, including two-headed animals, a unicorn, and other animal oddities.

Proceeding with the caveat that one or both prints could be fakes from known (but misidentified) animals, from chupacabras, or even from some other unknown animals, I derived a set of tracks (figs. 15A and 15B) based upon the photographs and showed them to Fernando.

Fernando carefully examined both sets of tracks. "I have never seen tracks like these here in the jungle," he said. "The nearest match for the smaller track is that of a *mapachin*." He pulled a laminated animal field guide out of his small tan backpack and pointed to an illustration of a *mapachin*. As with many jungle animals, it is known by different names including *zualasti* and *suksuk*, though its scientific name is *Procyon lotor*; in English it is called a raccoon. Could a juvenile chupacabra leave tracks that resembled those of a raccoon? It is certainly possible, since descriptions of the creature's size and characteristics vary so widely. (In fact, at least one dead raccoon, in Wise County, Texas, was thought to be the chupacabra; see chapter 5.)

Figures 15A and 15B. A pair of tracks derived from two alleged chupacabra specimens. Illustrations by the author.

I asked Fernando what he thought of the larger and more intriguing Track (fig. 15A).

"This, I also have not seen, but the closest track is that of a *caucel*." The *caucel*, known in English as the margay (subspecies *Leopardus wiedii nicaraguae*), is a spotted cat weighing up to twenty pounds that can reach four and one-half feet from tip to tail. The margay is an excellent climber and spends much of its time in trees—part of the reason that its tracks are uncommon. Fernando agreed to lead our search for the chupacabra tracks the next morning.

That night in our hut Chris spoke again of strange dreams. He felt we were being stalked or watched, not only at night, or in the jungle, but more or less constantly. Having a background in psychology, I chalked it up to the heat, exhaustion, and chupacabra stories playing with our imaginations.

However, as I thought about it more, I realized there was a likely pharmaceutical culprit. Our antimalaria medication, Lariam, has unsettling side effects including horrific hallucinations, insomnia, vertigo, paranoia, and vivid nightmares. One or both of us would wake up in a cold sweat, relieved to find ourselves in a thatched jungle hut instead of facing some hyperrealistic nightmare from our slumbering subconscious: vivid sensations of burning wax or the breath of reptiles. My father, who had not taken the pills, slept soundly throughout the trip and reported no ill effects.

Drug enhanced or not, my fevered dreams were visions of the chupacabra, perhaps lurking mere meters away, cloaked in the jungle night. Perhaps not existing at all, merely a Hispanic boogeyman fable created to spook ranchers, frighten children, and confound investigators. It was partly this intriguing, frustrating mystery that kept me from a sound sleep.

Day 4: Finding the Chupacabra

The third morning began much like the first, in predawn darkness. After gathering our gear and choking down a quick breakfast of bland granola bars and a drink box of warm pineapple juice, we headed out. After searching miles of jungle trails, we returned to camp, had lunch, and joined Fernando for another expedition in search of chupacabra tracks.

For hours Fernando guided us on (and off) the trails, pointing out flora, fauna, and tracks. He explained that he could get a very accurate picture of the animal from just a few tracks, including its size, weight, sex, and age, along

Figure 16. Guide Fernando Casanova and the author examine tracks in mud at the Indio Maiz Biological Reserve. Photo by Chris Ayles.

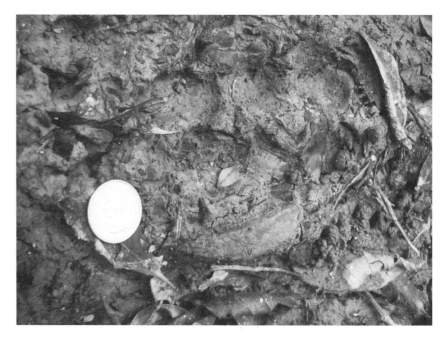

Figure 17. Mysterious track: jaguar or chupacabra? Photo by the author.

with the direction and speed of its travel. After a few minutes it was clear that Fernando's tracking skills were uncanny. At one point on a riverbed he stopped in mid-stride, looked to his left, walked over a few feet, and then looked under a large leaf to reveal a print in the mud. He pointed to the track and used both hands to indicate the size of the animal that left the track.

I walked over carefully for a closer look. "Could this be chupacabra?" I asked.

"No. It is a little like the drawing you showed me, but different. This is jaguar, the animal was here maybe twenty days ago."

A few minutes later, we found another jaguar track (fig. 17), this one smaller and much more recent—only five or six days old. We also found pig, tapir, raccoon, and others. The rest of the day we followed monkeys, searched for tracks, and recorded observations.

That evening we dined on beans, rice, spaghetti, and salad. Over our last evening meal, the three of us reflected on our expedition. We had succeeded in finding many fascinating animals (the monkeys were a particular favorite), but no chupacabra. Our expedition was running short of both time and supplies, and so far we hadn't found any evidence at all that would justify staying longer or pressing further.

That night Chris and I stayed up later than usual, inside our hut packing bags in preparation for the next day's midday departure. As we chatted, I heard a familiar noise above. Chris heard it too. I played the light around, but saw nothing. I knew something was there, but it seemed invisible. I could hear it, almost feel it, but couldn't see it. Being naturally skeptical of invisible creatures, I assumed that it was moving too quickly for my flashlight to catch, and the ambient light was too dim for my eyes.

On a hunch, I took out a digital camera from my pack and took a quick series of flash photographs in the air all around the room. Most of them were out of focus or revealed only wooden support poles. But I did capture one image of the creature that had been flying above our beds and invading our dreams. The chupacabras of my nightmares did not reside in my imagination, but in the thatched roof above. It may have been an insectivore, or it may have been a bloodsucker, but it was certainly a bat. In fact there were now two. We laughed uneasily and finished packing while the bats circled a few feet overhead. The spooky sound that had puzzled and terrified us for three nights remained, but the once-fearsome flapping was now almost calming.

Figure 18. One of several bats living in the thatch above the beds in cabins at the Indio Maiz Biopark. Photo by the author.

While our search for the legendary chupacabra had failed to yield solid results, we had indeed found a chupacabra—in fact more than one. The jungle does harbor bloodsucking animals, including of course the female mosquito, freshwater leeches, and vampire bats. There were undoubtedly *chupavacas* (cowsuckers) in the area, and likely *chupaperros* (dogsuckers), though the "official" chupacabra was a no-show.

Do chupacabras lurk somewhere in Nicaragua? Possibly, but the results from this expedition argue against it. Despite searching in one of the most likely spots in the world to find chupacabras, there seemed to be no evidence of them. No sightings, no tracks, no reports of their signature style of predation.

Of course, as with anything, absence of evidence is not evidence of absence; it's always possible that every single search (mine and all the others) was simply looking at the wrong place or at the wrong time. No matter how many times Loch Ness is searched (and no matter how thoroughly), people will still believe that Nessie lives in the lake. The history of cryptozoology is riddled with dozens of expeditions and searches to find such mystery animals, and the perpetual lack of hard evidence seems to have little effect on popular belief in the creatures.

Just as chupacabras seem to have disappeared from Puerto Rico over the past decade, it seems that the creatures are gone from Nicaragua as well. In recent years the most high-profile sightings have occurred in the United States. If the chupacabra is (or was) a real animal, the scarcity and pattern of sightings suggest that it is almost certainly near extinction.

The Dead Vampires Speak
Chupacabra Carcasses

Though I did not find a chupacabra (live or dead) during my expedition in Nicaragua, others have been far more fortunate (if one can call finding a putrefying monster carcass "fortunate"). In fact, about a half-dozen alleged chupacabras have been seen alive or found dead, most of them since 2000 and in North America. These chupacabras give unique insight into the nature of the chupacabra—not only as a would-be flesh-and-blood animal, but more importantly as a social and cultural phenomenon.

This chapter provides an objective overview of the best-known and best-researched chupacabra incidents on record, in chronological order. Since the vast majority of chupacabra reports leave little or no physical trace, these cases represent the best hard evidence for the mysterious creatures. In contrast to the idea that "dead men tell no tales," with modern forensic science often dead men—and dead chupacabras—have much to say. I personally investigated all but two of these cases, and my research into the most famous chupacabra ever found, by rancher Phylis Canion of Cuero, Texas, is fully treated in chapter 6.

Talavera's Terror: Malpaisillo, Nicaragua, 2000

Though the chupacabra had been sighted many times since its Puerto Rican appearance in 1995, there were only unconfirmed rumors about the recovery of any actual chupacabra bodies. There was no shortage of reported chupacabra *victims*—quite the contrary, the vampiric beasts had supposedly left enough blood-drained animals to fill a small (albeit anemic and not terribly interesting) zoo. Just when it seemed that the creature would never be found—and therefore more or less confirmed as a myth—a chupacabra was recovered.

It happened on a small farm in Nicaragua. In late August 2000, farmer Jorge Talavera had suffered the loss of some of his livestock. Recently the animal killings had increased, along with an odd twist—many of the animals appeared to have been bled dry. "In fifteen days it sucked twenty-five sheep, and my neighbor lost thirty-five sheep in ten days," Talavera said. "It was an average of five sheep and goats a night." Exasperated at finding dead animals on his farm, Talavera resolved to kill whatever was draining his animals' blood—and his livelihood.

On the evening of August 25, Talavera and a friend staked out his ranch to catch the mysterious predator. After several idle hours watching over his animals, Talavera heard the alarmed cry of a goat, and in the near-darkness saw a most bizarre sight: two (or possibly three) unknown creatures among his flock of goats. Talavera described them as having the head of a bull; rose-colored teeth; the hairless, leathery skin of a bat; and a bumpy, crocodile-like crest down its spine (Greste 2000). The creatures—one or two black ones and a yellow one—reared up on their hind legs to attack the goats. (A later account further described it as having "yellow hair on its short tail, large eye-sockets . . . and large claws and fangs.")

Talavera opened fire on the suspected chupacabras with a shotgun: "We shot at them in the distance. We hit one and wounded it, but they both ran away before we could catch them, losing them in the darkness." The next day Talavera searched for the strange creatures, but was unable to find any trace of them.

Three days later while tending to chores, a ranch hand named Jairo Garcia noticed vultures circling in the distance, apparently having located some carrion. Curious, he followed the birds to the mouth of a small cave (or "cave-like structure"—accounts vary) near the farm, where he discovered the near-skeletal remains of the putrid beast. Much of its body had been eaten, and the remains were in an advanced state of decomposition.

According to one account (Vergara 2000), "What Don Jairo [Mr. Garcia] found most startling was the lack of bodily hair and very small ears. Although the animal had been reduced to a skeleton after the vultures feasted upon it, it was shaped like a long, yellow-colored dog, given the pigmentation which could still be seen on part of its tail." Convinced that "he found the animal his employer had shot two nights earlier and which was probably responsible for the deaths of so many sheep," Garcia summoned Talavera to see for himself, and they concluded that they had made history by finally killing the elusive chupacabra.

Within days, Talavera's find made national, then international news as word spread and journalists got wind of the story (Pilkington 2000). Rumors soon swirled around the case like flies on a dead goat. Some believed the beast had escaped from a traveling circus; others said it might be a previously unknown creature from darkest Africa. A local veterinarian, Giocconda Chevez, speculated that "the creature could be a hybrid of several species, created in a laboratory by means of genetic engineering." Many believed it was an otherwise ordinary dog that had somehow developed a thirst for blood (and presumably the ability to suck it); one creative person speculated it might be a cross between a wolf and a crocodile.

Rev. Francisco Ortiz, head of a Pentecostal church in nearby Leon, stated that he believed the mystery beast might be a sign that the End Times were near. Ortiz told his followers that it was "a warning sign . . . a sign for men and women to return to God because we've forgotten about him." Ortiz cited Bible scripture (particularly the Book of Daniel) to prove his case.

Whatever it was—mutant hybrid, genetic experiment, Armageddon portent, or chupacabra—most people in the small community were relieved the menace had been killed. The remains were taken to the local university, the National Autonomous University of Nicaragua (UNAN), where biologist Pedrarias Dávila examined the body: "We recorded the characteristics of the skeletal system, number of vertebrae and ribs, nails, decomposition state, among others, to place it in a database." He was unable to make an immediate identification of the skeleton, except to say that he was convinced it was a mammal. Two days later, Dávila issued a statement saying that his forensics team had so far found nothing unusual about the skeleton: "The anatomic detail sheds no anomalous information. We see a complete bone structure, a well-formed spinal column resembling that of a canine, and from what we have ascertained, it isn't a hematophagous or blood sucking animal" (quoted in Vergara 2000). As the scientists carried out their work, gawkers and curiosity seekers, hoping for a glimpse of the infamous chupacabra, disrupted the local hospital morgue, while journalists called seeking comment and wanting to photograph the find of the century.

On September 6, the UNAN scientists concluded their examination; zoologist Edmundo Torres stated what many had long suspected: "It's a dog, without any room for doubt. This is a common dog. There are no fangs or anything that could suck blood" (Knight-Ridder 2000). If it appeared odd, it likely had mange or another skin disease.

This verdict did not sit well with Talavera, who by now was enjoying his nominal fame as the local chupacabra slayer. Though he acknowledged that it resembled a dog, he insisted it could not be a canine because "its teeth were pink in color, it stood differently, and it drained the blood of at least 120 sheep." In fact, not only did Talavera dispute the university's findings, but when presented with his bones, the case took a surprising twist: he accused the scientists of a conspiracy and cover-up.

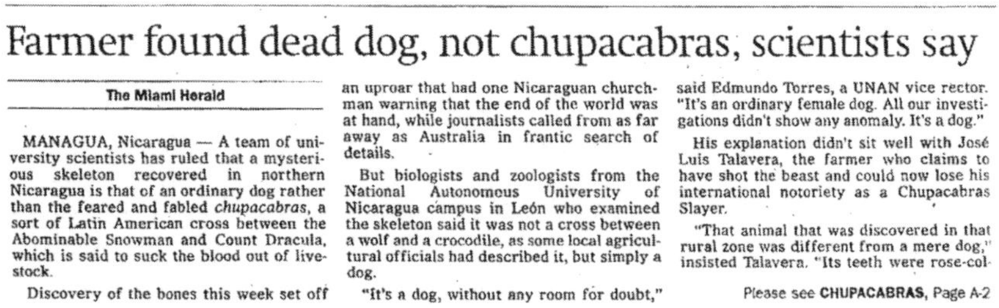

Farmer found dead dog, not chupacabras, scientists say

The Miami Herald

MANAGUA, Nicaragua — A team of university scientists has ruled that a mysterious skeleton recovered in northern Nicaragua is that of an ordinary dog rather than the feared and fabled *chupacabras*, a sort of Latin American cross between the Abominable Snowman and Count Dracula, which is said to suck the blood out of livestock.

Discovery of the bones this week set off an uproar that had one Nicaraguan churchman warning that the end of the world was at hand, while journalists called from as far away as Australia in frantic search of details.

But biologists and zoologists from the National Autonomous University of Nicaragua campus in León who examined the skeleton said it was not a cross between a wolf and a crocodile, as some local agricultural officials had described it, but simply a dog.

"It's a dog, without any room for doubt," said Edmundo Torres, a UNAN vice rector. "It's an ordinary female dog. All our investigations didn't show any anomaly. It's a dog."

His explanation didn't sit well with José Luis Talavera, the farmer who claims to have shot the beast and could now lose his international notoriety as a Chupacabras Slayer.

"That animal that was discovered in that rural zone was different from a mere dog," insisted Talavera. "Its teeth were rose-col-

Please see **CHUPACABRAS**, *Page A-2*

Figure 19. A newspaper headline reveals the results from a suspected chupacabra found in Malpaisillo, Nicaragua.

"That animal was switched around at the university," Talavera claimed. The real chupacabra he had shot on August 25 had been secretly switched for unknown, nefarious purposes. According to the daily newspaper *La Prensa de Nicaragua* (2000), "Talavera claims that there are several pieces of evidence that prove that the skeleton was indeed changed at the UNAN-Leon's laboratory. The first of these is that 'the skeleton is complete, although I kept a piece of its front leg.' He also claims that the bones turned from a dark color to a lighter one, the teeth turned from pink to white, and from twenty-two teeth that he counted there are now forty, as well as 'more skin on the legs'" ("This Isn't My Goatsucker!" 2000).

UNAN scientists, clearly annoyed by both the media circus and Talavera's dogged insistence of a cover-up, dismissed his claim as paranoia. The teeth may have turned from bloodstained pink to white during cleaning, and the bones would have similarly lightened when the scientists removed the dirt and contamination for the forensic examination. Talavera seemed unable to offer any real proof for the other claims.

The university reiterated their offer to return the bones, but Talavera refused, not wanting to pay the transportation fees to collect the (allegedly switched) dog remains. Talavera later seemed to admit that perhaps his chupacabra had been a dog after all, but "even though it may have been a dog, it was an uncommon one, given that it fed on blood . . . the researchers left many questions unanswered, such as the cause of death and why it fed on blood." (It is important to note that Talavera never actually had his sheep autopsied to determine if in fact the animals had been drained of blood.)

Many seemed to accept the scientific analysis, though others in the community remained skeptical, including the mayor of Malpaisillo, Leonel Navarro. The issue soon faded away, and there were no further reports of any found carcasses.

Given that Talavera's only sighting of the chupacabra occurred at night, the accuracy of his original description is suspect. He did not state how far away he was from the chupacabra when he shot at it, but since he only hit one of the creatures it seems unlikely he was very close. His report of seeing such a specific detail as the color of the teeth on a moving creature at night from a distance would suggest he has remarkable (perhaps superhuman) vision—or a good imagination. There's also the question (which, in my study of all the reports, no one seems to have raised) of whether or not the creature that Talavera saw and shot at is necessarily the same creature whose carcass was found three days later at a different location, picked over by vultures. It seems at least possible that it was a different animal that had died there at another time. In fact, there is some evidence that it is not the same creature: the animal's skeleton (as can be seen in an episode of the National Geographic series *Is It Real?*) does not show evidence of gunshot wounds.

Then there's Talavera's interesting claim of skull skullduggery. While it is of course *possible* that the bones were switched by the university staff, there would seem to be little benefit or purpose to doing so. Aside from that, the university would have to have a dog skeleton on hand of just the right species, size, and shape to exchange for Talavera's chupacabra. If the skeleton were property of the university (such as a canine specimen in a collection), it would be marked as such on the bones themselves.

A Chupacabra Named Jenny: Rio Rancho, New Mexico, 2002

In 2002, on a sunbaked mesa on the outskirts of Albuquerque, New Mexico, a bizarre creature was found half buried in the rocks and sand. It wasn't a dog or a coyote. It wasn't a bird or a cow. In fact, it was unlike anything the finder had ever seen. The creature was dead but not rotting, nor was it a skeleton. Instead it was dried, almost as if the desert winds had carefully preserved the mystery. It had a vaguely human-like face, a pointy head, what seemed to be stubby wings, and a long tail. The man who found it passed it along to his friend Bob Wheeler, who kept the curiosity and occasionally showed it to his friends and family "to freak them out." One person thought it looked like a gargoyle; another suggested an alien. But Wheeler settled on his own identification: "[To people of] Spanish heritage, it's the chupacabra," Wheeler told a local TV station. "The goatsucker is what they call it" (Upton 2005).

Three years later, in February 2005, the world's second alleged chupacabra body came to national attention when one of Wheeler's friends suggested that he ought to have professionals identify the creature. The remains were taken to Brian Gleadle of New Mexico's Department of Game and Fish. *Rio Rancho Journal* reporter Barbara Armijo reported the results on February 12: "A creepy-looking skeleton found on the West Mesa several years ago is not the remains of the dreaded chupacabra, a mythical creature said to suck the blood from goats" (Armijo 2005).

Instead of a chupacabra, Gleadle said, the bizarre creature is a skate, an animal related to stingrays. Yet Gleadle's explanation doesn't complete the story, for he didn't fully identify the crusty creature either. Gleadle offered an opinion as to the object's origin: "It's common for a slice of the actual wing to be used as a food source, and that's what we believe was the case with this one. . . . Someone had to have caught it in the ocean, most likely the Gulf of Mexico. They then probably cut the part that was edible and tossed the rest."

Whether skate or chupacabra, the story (if not the beast) had legs. Some mystery-mongering websites (such as unexplainedresearch.com and unexplainable.net) were quick to post stories and images of the creature, and it made the local news. One local television station, KOB-TV, noted, "After doing some research, Eyewitness News 4 has concluded that the creature probably lived in the ocean at one time and probably isn't either a chupacabra or an alien" (Upton 2005; Dukart 2005).

When I saw the newspaper's photograph of the ex-chupacabra, I immediately recognized it as a Devil Fish, also known as a Jenny Haniver (Radford 2007). It is in fact a cut-up, deformed, and carefully dried skate; it was created

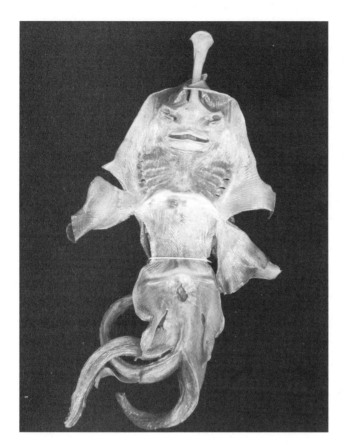

Figure 20.
A suspected chupacabra identical to one found outside Albuquerque, New Mexico. From the author's collection, photo by the author.

as an oddity—essentially a faked monster. Jenny Hanivers date back over three hundred years, and are sold in curio shops around the world but especially in the Caribbean (for more on Jenny Hanivers, see Eberhart 2002, 106, 109; Dance 1975). I have seen dozens of them in carnival sideshows and exhibits.

But why did an ocean animal end up on a desert mesa? A clue can be found in the newspaper's photograph. The left "leg" of Wheeler's creature was broken off at the "knee," which probably explains why it was thrown away. The skate was never used for food; it would not have been specifically formed into a Jenny Haniver, nor would it have been so well preserved if that had been the case. It was merely a damaged curio item, tossed out on the mesa instead of in the dump. Wheeler's (mis)identification of the Jenny Haniver as a chupacabra is instructive (and, as we will see, typical), since the remains look nothing like the typical descriptions of the vampiric beast.

The Elmendorf Beast: Elmendorf, Texas, 2004

Devin McAnally, a retired teacher and rancher in the town of Elmendorf, Texas, noticed a strange animal eating mulberries under a tree on his property around May 20, 2004. The thin creature had large ears and a bluish cast, and was nearly hairless. Suspecting that the creature had earlier attacked his livestock, McAnally shot the animal.

Figure 21. A sketch of the chupacabra shot by Devin McAnally in Elmendorf, Texas. Sketch by the author.

Upon closer inspection, he saw that the creature was a twenty-pound female, possibly pregnant. McAnally later wrote,

> Only a narrow ridge of quarter-inch-long blue hair edged both sides of her spine from the base of her tail to the tip of her shoulders at her neck. Her wrinkled skin immediately made me think of an elephant's. Her skin was a sky-blue cast, light gray color, with a slight whitish marbling in her hip and flank areas. Her ears weren't pointed like a fox's or even a coyote's; they were shaped more rounded, like a cat's. She had a long tail, about 18 inches, nearly as long as her trunk, about 20 inches. Her snout was exceptionally long and rat-like. Her jaw revealed four incisor teeth: two upper

and two lower that protruded outside her lips, like a wild pig's. (McAnally 2009a)

"I have lived here for fifteen years and have never seen anything like it," he told Elvia Aguilar of the *San Antonio Express-News* (Aguilar 2004). Before burying the carcass in his yard, he pried out one of its teeth and submitted it for DNA analysis to New York University.

According to McAnally,

> I shot and killed the strange animal that would become the very first authentic specimen of the storied chupacabra. . . . I am not the first person to see a chupacabra alive, nor am I the first to find a dead one or even to kill one. However, I was lucky enough, or had accumulated enough bad karma, to shoot one, photograph it, preserve what I could of the remains, and to make it available for factual, natural science analytical investigations. I very much regret killing the animal, despite the damage it did to my poultry, but I would be much more selective in the public institutions and persons I trusted if I had it to do all over again. And I would do it all over again, feeling as I do that somehow God gave me a chance to use the chupacabra discovery to help me develop my little ranch on the San Antonio River as a second-chance home for children and adolescents. (McAnally 2009a)

As would become typical with curious creatures found in the Lone Star State, some thought the beast was a chupacabra. An official from the San Antonio Zoo suspected the animal might be a wild Mexican dog: "It's clearly a member of the dog family, a family Canidae." Wildlife biologist Brian Mesenbrink looked at McAnally's photographs and concluded it was probably a coyote with mange, noting that the area has a large population of coyotes (McAnally disputes the diagnosis of mange). Because of the animal's distinctive overbite, some thought the animal might be a Muntjac deer. Others speculated that it was an odd hybrid of wolf, coyote, or dog. For his part, McAnally hoped "that this supposed blood-sucker is actually a very unique part of our natural world, a New World canine, thus far hidden from European explorers and settlers . . ." (He told me he eventually got hate mail and disturbing, anonymous phone calls accusing him of killing "one of Nature's rarest creatures" [McAnally 2009b].)

Professor Todd Disotell of New York University contacted McAnally with the results weeks later. Disotell wrote, "The DNA was quite degraded, presumably due to exposure to the elements and heat, but nonetheless 138 bp of the mitochondrial 16s rRNA region were sequenced. No nuclear DNA was obtainable." Disotell listed the GATC [genetic] sequence, concluding that "this sequence is not compatible with the subject being a coyote, *Canis lupus latrans*, and is in fact identical to the sequences of dozens of breeds of domestic dog, *Canis lupus familiaris*. The actual breed could not be determined from the short sequence" (Disotell 2004).

Thus scientific analysis proved that the Elmendorf Beast was in fact a common dog, probably stricken with mange. Significantly, McAnally did not report that any of his animals had been mysteriously drained of blood—just that they had been the victim of ordinary predation (McAnally 2009b). This omission would of course suggest that the animal was not in fact a chupacabra, and together with the DNA analysis essentially puts the matter to rest.[1]

The Maine Beast: Turner, Maine, 2006

While the vast majority of found chupacabras in the United States come from New Mexico or Texas, occasionally they are seen farther north. For years, Maine residents have reported occasional sightings of a mysterious creature with a bloodcurdling cry and glowing eyes. The beast is said to attack and kill pets, especially dogs. The animal is elusive, always evading attempts to track, capture, or kill it.

That is, apparently, until August 12, 2006, when a woman in the town of Turner, Maine, found a strange dead animal. The creature appeared mostly blue; it had blue eyes, blue lips, and charcoal-colored fur. Though it had four legs and resembled a dog, Michelle O'Donnell, a neighbor, was certain that the creature was not a dog. Sensing that she had an amazing find—perhaps even a long-sought mystery beast—she took photos of it that were published in the local newspaper and posted online. While flies swirled around the decaying carcass, controversy swirled around O'Donnell's photographs.

The "Maine Monster" was a media sensation, making international news and spawning speculation. While some claimed that the animal was a chupacabra (or, as in the 2000 Nicaraguan chupacabra case, an unspecified "mutant hybrid"), others suspected it was just an unusual-looking dog. Finally a sample of the creature was sent to the University of Maine, where DNA analysis concluded that the animal's mother was from the *Canis* family. While the father's genetic link was not absolutely certain, it was likely also a *Canis*. According to

University of Maine scientist Irv Kornfield, the beast "has all the indicators to link it to being from *Canis*, a dog" (Radford 2006).

Thus the matter was settled, for all but the most die-hard of believers. If the animal had just been glimpsed as it bounded into a wooded area and not caught (or later found dead), it would remain a mystery monster to be written up in future books on the unexplained. Instead, another chupacabra—the third in six years—was identified as a dog.

El Chupacabra de La Luz: Albuquerque, New Mexico, 2007

The chupacabra reared its ugly, bloodsucking head in New Mexico in early September 2007. The beast was reported along Coors Road, on the West Mesa of Albuquerque, not far from the woods of the Rio Grande. Two residents from an apartment complex called La Luz (the light) saw a bizarre, four-legged creature among the sand dunes and scrub brush in the fields nearby (fig. 23). It resembled a dog or coyote, but was unlike anything Wendy Kalberg had ever seen. "Its tail was very slight and thin," she said, and it had huge ears, and "sores on it, or scars on it also" (Maestas 2007).

Kalberg and her (anonymous) neighbor were frightened by the animal, but were even more curious about what it was: "Everybody I've described it to has said, 'Is it a chupacabra?'" While Kalberg said she didn't believe the chupacabra exists, her neighbor was wary: "From reading about chupacabra descriptions and how vicious it is, we quit walking [around the area]." Other residents took extra precautions and kept their animals inside, just to be safe.

Figure 22. Area along Coors Rd. in Albuquerque, New Mexico, where a chupacabra was sighted in 2007. Photo by the author.

Figure 23. Image of the Coors Rd. chupacabra. Screen shot from KRQE news report.

The pair agreed to keep an eye out the window for the beast, and about a week later, Kalberg's neighbor spotted the creature again—this time from the safety of her car, and she had a camera with her. "He was about ten feet away, and I stopped the car and began taking pictures," she said. The chupacabra posed just long enough for some snapshots, then scampered away. The pair sent the photographs to the Albuquerque Zoo, hoping that someone there could help solve the mystery.

At first the zoo wasn't sure what to make of the photos—or even who to pass them along to. Rick Janser, the zoo manager, had no idea what it was. Having the actual animal in front of him would make identifying the creature much easier, but a photo would have to do.

His first impression? "This is scary looking," he said. "Definitely strange. Really pointy, elongated snout." He ran through the likely possibilities, including coyotes (which are common in the area, and often responsible for missing pets), foxes, and dogs. He suspected it was some unusual breed of dog, and research soon confirmed his hunch. "We checked it out, and it's a breed from Mexico that's specifically bred in Mexico," Janser said (Maestas 2007).

The breed is called Xoloitzcuintli, but for obvious reasons is often simply called a Xolo ("Zolo"). The Xolo is an ancient breed, and has lived in Mexico for at least three thousand years; the earliest are believed to be a hairless mutation of native Indian breeds (Cahoon 2008). It's little wonder that few people recognized the animal, given the breed's rarity and the animal's poor health. The Chupacabra de La Luz was never caught; it likely died of disease or malnutrition somewhere out on the mesa or in the woods near the Rio Grande.

The Butler/Ayer Chupacabra: Blanco, Texas, 2009

In late July 2009 (the exact date is unclear) a man living near the small wind-swept town of Blanco, Texas, heard chickens in his barn being harassed or attacked by some animal. The creature escaped before he could catch it (or even catch a glimpse of it). Assuming the beast was a raccoon or other varmint, he left poison for it.

The next morning he discovered a dead animal unlike any he'd ever seen, a beast many would come to call a chupacabra. It weighed about eighty pounds and was obviously a canid, resembling a coyote or dog—though its front legs were a few inches longer than most coyotes'. Its skin was a dark chocolate color, and mostly hairless except for around the feet and along its backbone.

He contacted his cousin, Lynn Butler, who also didn't know what to make of the strange creature. They put it in a freezer, and Butler decided that the person most likely to identify the creature was Jerry Ayer, a friend of his and a local taxidermist of twenty years' experience.

"One of my former students called me up and kind of jokingly said, 'Hey, I've got a chupacabra!' I looked at it and thought, 'Hey, that's weird looking,'"

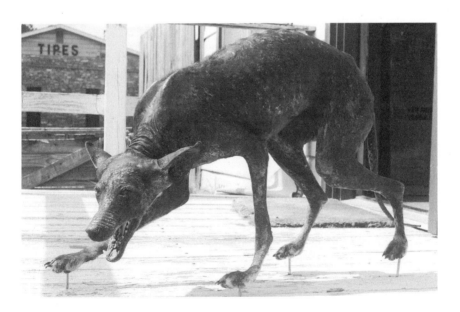

Figure 24. Chupacabra found near Blanco, Texas, and mounted by Jerry Ayer. Photo courtesy of Jerry Ayer.

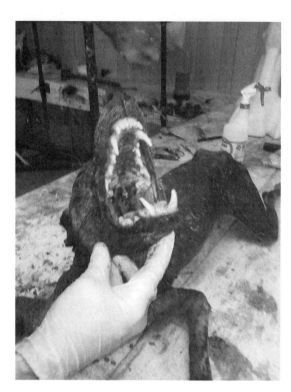

Figure 25. The fearsome teeth and jaws of the Blanco chupacabra, seen as it was being prepared for taxidermy. Photo courtesy of Jerry Ayer.

Ayer told me. "My wheels started spinning when I saw this animal because I knew immediately that it was the same animal that had been seen in Cuero, and they had labeled it the chupacabra." (See next chapter for the whole story of the Cuero chupacabra.)

Ayer asked Butler what he planned to do with the carcass, and Butler told him "he didn't want to have anything to do with it, and asked if I'd be willing to trade it for a course I teach on duck taxidermy. So I traded him a duck course for the chupacabra. Before he sent it to me, he had [officers from] Fish and Wildlife come out to see what he had, make sure he wasn't doing anything wrong. They scratched their heads and said they didn't know what the heck it was. Then Texas A&M came out, and they took samples from the body."

Examining the Blanco Chupacabra

Public opinion about the mysterious beast was divided into three camps. The first (and obviously most popular) explanation was that the animal was in fact the long-sought chupacabra—finally captured (though poisoned) and finally available for scientific inquiry. The second two suggestions were much more skeptical and mundane: the animal was either a Xolo dog (mentioned earlier in this chapter) or a mangy coyote.

Jerry Ayer is the first person known to have dissected an alleged chupacabra for taxidermy purposes. "It's very coyote-like, it resembles the shape of the coyote, it's got canine teeth, and the basic skeletal structure of a coyote. But I don't believe it's a Xolo dog, and I don't necessarily believe it's just a coyote with a bad case of mange. The Xolo dogs look very similar. But what I have not witnessed on those dogs is the coyote hair. Now, this thing is hairless—95 percent of it. It has a little bit of hair, like right between the shoulder blades, and that hair was a blend of blond, brown, and black, which is identical to coyote hair. It looks like coyote hair to me.

"I tend to not think it's just a coyote with a bad case of mange," Ayer told me. "I've had a lot of photos sent to me of coyotes with bad mange, and they looked similar, but they all tended to have more hair. Yes, they were bald in lots of spots, but they had big chunks of hair in certain spots. I haven't seen any that were almost completely bald like this one" (Ayer 2009).

So is it a chupacabra? Ayer didn't think so. "I don't believe in chupacabras," Ayer said emphatically. "I don't believe in any mythical beasts whatsoever. We labeled it that because everyone else was calling it that. . . . To be honest, I don't know what it is. I'd probably say it's a freak-of-nature coyote, or a hybrid breed with a genetic mutation. It doesn't matter what I call it, it's been labeled [by the community and press] . . . People say there's a mythical beast and [that] I have one. I'll call it chupacabra because people love it, but I don't know what it is" (Pierce 2009).

Ayer was refreshingly (and unusually) candid with me about the limits of his expertise, wary of having been misquoted by several journalists who made it seem as though he had authenticated the chupacabra. "I'm not a scientist or anything, and I don't have the DNA results back, it's just my opinion. I know what my limitations are. I'm a taxidermist, and I'm good at identifying lots of animals, it is part of my job, but when something comes into my possession that I don't know, there's no way I can jump out on a limb and start claiming that it's this or that."

The Blanco Chupacabra Finds a Home

As Ayer finished stuffing and mounting the chupacabra, the media blitz became overwhelming. The news got out, and soon the taxidermy school where Ayer works was getting nearly one hundred calls a day from people all over the world wanting to see the chupacabra. He fielded interview requests from CNN, *Good Morning America*, and Indonesian radio. Gawkers stopped by his shop. Ayer soon grew weary of the press blitz, wanting the creature out of his shop and the relentless media out of his life. "I took it figuring I could get some publicity for the shop out of it, and overnight it pretty much just blew up. It went from Miami to Chicago to LA in basically twenty-four hours. I got flooded with e-mails and phone calls and everything, and I soon decided I should get it mounted and out of my possession as quickly as possible because it was getting kind of crazy. In the beginning of course I wanted to do it for publicity, but I just didn't realize it would take off like it did." (Ayer turned down the *Good Morning America* gig, saying, "I didn't feel like going to New York City to talk about a mythical creature on national television.")

Figure 26. Jerry Ayer shows off his taxidermy skills on the Blanco chupacabra. Photo courtesy of Jerry Ayer.

Not all of the visitors and callers wanted to see his chupacabra; many wanted to buy it. Ayer fielded dozens of offers to buy the beast, but finally it was sold on September 18, 2009, for an undisclosed sum (likely well above $5,000) to a real estate agent and part-time curator named John Adolfi as part of a collection for his museum in the small town of Phoenix, New York.

In fact, the beast was displayed in an exclusive engagement (titled rather unimaginatively "The Chupacabra Exhibit") during October 2009 as an example of the fallibility of science at the creationist Lost World Museum. (For more on the link between fundamentalist Christian theology and the chupacabra, see chapter 3.)

Ayer had higher offers, but felt that Adolfi's museum would be a good fit. "I thought it was an interesting place, I thought Wow, he's going to go ahead and try to compare Intelligent Design, Christianity, creationism and evolution . . . It's like oil and water, things that don't mix real well. I figured, hey, this will be a great thing for him to put up there with his one-eyed cat or whatever."

The Non-Chupa, Non-Cabra

Indications that the Blanco chupacabra was perhaps not particularly mysterious were clear from the beginning. A closer look at the circumstances of the animal's discovery suggests nothing unusual about the find—there was in fact no reason to think that the animal was a chupacabra in the first place, no indication of the chupacabra's signature attack: blood mysteriously drained from chickens, goats, or other livestock. The circumstances are completely unlike that of the chupacabra, and entirely consistent with an ordinary dog or coyote attack. I asked Ayer if he knew of any vampiric element to the story: "In all the reports, I didn't see any mention of anyone saying that whatever attacked the chickens drained any blood. Did that happen?"

"No," he said. "Not at all, we don't know anything about that, all Lynn's cousin knew is that the animal was tearing up animals in his barn, so he put poison out . . . There was no witness of any kind of bloodsucking going on; I don't even believe that any livestock was harmed, I never heard of anything like that. No dead animals or evidence of distressed livestock that this thing had attacked, none of that at all, whatsoever."

So not only were the chickens *not* mysteriously drained of blood, they weren't even harmed! The chickens were simply harassed, perhaps chased around the barn, by the alleged chupacabra. Furthermore, as in the Talavera sighting in Nicaragua, it's not certain that the animal that originally bothered the chickens was the same beast that succumbed to the poison. It seems likely, but since the chicken attacker was never seen, it is possible that a second animal (perhaps a sick and mangy coyote) might have wandered into the barn after the first animal had been chased off hours earlier.

The only reason anyone suspected the animal was a chupacabra was that it looked unusual, and seemed to have even less hair than Ayer expected from a coyote with mange. Of course, while members of a particular species will exhibit similar morphological traits, there can be significant individual variation within the species, and even within the subspecies. Just as some men are bald while others have a full head of hair, animals can also vary significantly between individuals.

And some canids, like all other animals, may be deformed by nonfatal birth defects, accident, injury, or disease. The same is true for the effects of a given disease. A dog or coyote that is suffering from malnutrition and in the advanced stages of mange may look different even from one in earlier stages. Comparing a given animal to what a person thinks the typical specimen "should" look like is not a reliable gauge as to whether or not it is a hybrid or a new creature.

As this book went to press, DNA results about this very coyote-like chupacabra had apparently not been conducted—or if they were, the results have not been made public. Jerry Ayer told me that he was not in contact with anyone who took DNA samples, and suggested I contact the man he sold it to, John Adolfi at the Lost World Museum. When I contacted Adolfi to ask what had become of the chupacabra flesh specimens I was told, "The samples were not collected like I had hoped through us. Jerry Ayers [sic] supposedly had some samples taken and he may know more about it than we" (Adolfi 2010). Adolfi, of course, could submit a small sample of his beast to scientific analysis at any time. If the animal on display as a chupacabra actually is one, Adolfi does not seem particularly interested in obtaining DNA evidence that would prove it.

The Lake Bridgeport Chupacabra: Wise County, Texas, 2010

Tony Potter, a maintenance worker at a golf course in Runaway Bay, an hour north of Fort Worth, Texas, came across a bizarre sight while beginning work on the otherwise ordinary morning of January 13, 2010. He found a small, strange, four-legged animal that was mostly hairless, with tan-brown skin. It didn't look like anything Potter had ever seen before: "I get out here and

Figure 27. This strange, mostly hairless chupacabra was found near Runaway Bay, Texas. Photo courtesy of the *Wise County Messenger*.

I was like, 'What is that? It's not a dog.'" He showed it to a local veterinarian, who couldn't identify the curious creature, so Potter posted a video of it on YouTube. Some thought it was a hairless dog. Others thought it must be another Texas chupacabra—an identification that, of course, stuck. Was it the legendary goatsucker, as many people suggested?

Potter himself didn't think so; in fact he suspected it was a hairless raccoon. Jennifer Barrow, a biologist with the Texas Parks and Wildlife Department, examined the carcass and concluded that Potter was correct: it was a young male raccoon. "It was a raccoon, no doubt about it. Its feet were a real giveaway. It had long toes, narrow feet . . . everything right for a raccoon." But Barrow didn't stop there. She also compared the animal's teeth and skull to that of a comparison specimen raccoon skull. They matched: "This tooth right here is this tooth right here," Barrow demonstrated for reporter Jim Douglas of WFAA-TV. "It matches perfectly" (Douglas 2010).

The mystery soon turned from wondering if the animal was a chupacabra to why the unfortunate young raccoon had lost its fur. It didn't appear to have mange; Barrow noted that the animal's skin was very smooth, and thought it may have had a genetic disease that left it without hair. Or, Barrow speculated, the raccoon might have died when it fell into nearby

Lake Bridgeport and froze to death. The cold water might have caused the post-mortem hair loss (Miller 2010).

The identification of the chupacabra as a juvenile hairless raccoon more or less ended the issue, though for a few days in late January 2010, the small town of Bridgeport got national media attention for its chupacabra, and the citizens were quick to take advantage of the notoriety. Chupacabra-related T-shirts, hats, and promotions sprang up almost overnight, and even veterinarians at the local animal clinic put up a lighthearted sign offering to vaccinate chupacabras (Boie and Alvarado, 2010). Interestingly, this was not the first time that hairless raccoons had been mistaken for mysterious or unknown monsters; the so-called Montauk Monster, which was found along a shore near Long Island, was also identified as a raccoon (Radford 2009a; Radford 2010a).

The Horizon City Chupacabra: El Paso, Texas, 2010

In early 2010 another supposed chupacabra report surfaced in Horizon City, outside of El Paso, Texas. Even though a carcass was not recovered in this case, it is in many ways a textbook example of a typical present-day chupacabra report, complete with all the usual errors and mistaken assumptions. On the night of January 8, some animal attacked twenty chickens owned by a man named Cesar Garcia. Though no one saw the predatory animal, the

Figure 28. Three chickens lay dead following a suspected chupacabra attack in Horizon City, Texas. Photo courtesy of Jay Koester.

Figure 29. A chicken's bloody puncture wounds following a suspected chupacabra attack. Photos courtesy of Jay Koester.

attack puzzled Garcia because he expected to see more blood on the scene. "I saw the chickens were dead, but there was no blood around the sheet metal" in the coop. "All of them were just dead in one big pile. But, really, I don't know what it was because there was no blood. If it had been a dog, there would have been blood everywhere because a dog tears them apart," Garcia said. Note that Garcia did not claim that the chickens themselves had been drained of blood; in fact a photo accompanying the story showed a clearly bloody wound on a dead chicken (see fig. 29), and according to Jay Koester, the reporter who covered the story, "the chickens were still full of blood to my viewing."

Garcia was also baffled by the two holes he found on the necks of his chickens. When he did some searching on the Internet, he concluded that the wounds seemed similar to those left by the chupacabra (Koester 2010). The next evening, ten more chickens were found dead in a similar fashion in a different coop.

The elements are consistent, and by now the pattern should be instantly recognizable: An unseen animal kills some poultry or livestock; someone finds the victims and thinks that the deaths are mysterious or unusual for some reason; someone decides that there is less blood present that they were expecting (either in the victims' carcasses or outside them); he or she searches the web for "chupacabra" and finds photos or other information that "confirms" their encounter with the mysterious beast; and finally the local news media get wind of the story and report it with little or no skepticism. There is no scientific analysis, and whole chupacabra story is spun out of wild conjecture about a few dead chickens.

Part of the reason that chupacabra reports proliferate is that journalists and reporters are poorly informed about the subject. They don't know any more about the chupacabra than what they read on Wikipedia or glean from skimming a "believer" cryptozoology website. This ignorance is not entirely the reporters' fault; after all, it's an unusual subject in which credible, scientific analyses and authorities are difficult to find (hopefully this book will change that). Journalists—even careful, well-intentioned ones—don't necessarily understand the complexities and nuances of the chupacabra phenomenon, and therefore don't know what questions to ask to form a complete story.

Texas, the Chupacabra Factory

Why do chupacabras seem to appear more often in Texas than in other states? One answer is that the state's geography, culture, and ecology combine to create excellent conditions for manufacturing chupacabras.

The geography of Texas offers a clue as to the origins of its chupacabras. It is perhaps no coincidence that at least one of the "chupacabras" found in Texas has turned out to be a Mexican hairless dog, since Texas has the longest border with Mexico. While the U.S. Border Patrol has significant success keeping out illegal Mexican immigrants, dogs, coyotes, and other animals pass more or less freely across the border. These are exactly the types of animals that are most likely to be interpreted as chupacabras. Feral dogs and coyotes must feed on something, and the many ranches and farms in Texas provide an obvious food source. Especially with global temperatures increasing, the harsh desert terrain may drive animals to prey on creatures they might not otherwise attack.

There's also a biological reason for the prevalence of chupacabra reports in Texas. Mike Bowdenchuck, state director for Texas Wildlife Services, explained why wild animals with severe cases of mange are more common in Texas and the Southwest than in other rural areas: "Down here, animals don't die of mange, because the temperatures are warm enough. Mange is very common in colder areas; in fact wolves are getting it in Montana right now, and in North Dakota foxes get it. Up there it's fatal, so you never see animals with the severe cases that we see in the southern climates, because they don't live long enough for the mites to get that bad to cause the hair to fall off. They die of hypothermia first" (Bowdenchuck 2010). This piece of the puzzle fits perfectly: animals (legendary or otherwise) that have lost their fur would be more vulnerable to the elements, and therefore live longer (and be more likely to be seen) in warmer areas. If this is true, then sightings of animals with advanced stages of mange should be reported more often in northern areas as the climate warms (Radford 2010d).

And, of course, in order for someone to "identify" (rightly or wrongly) a strange animal as a chupacabra, there must be a preexisting knowledge of the beast. The Hispanic and Latin American cultural influences in Texas are stronger than in most other states, so the average Texan (especially one work-ing on a rural ranch) is far more likely to be aware of the chupacabra than is the average New Yorker or Oregonian.

Given the history of found chupacabras listed in this chapter, it is cer-tain that occasional chupacabra sightings will continue. The pattern is clear and unmistakable. Each new sighting will make national, maybe even inter-national, headlines (often accompanied by photos), crowing "Chupacabra Found!" The new dead beast and its owner will become a minor celebrity, hounded by press, gawkers, and a curious public. Samples of the animal's tis-sue may be submitted for analysis as doubts emerge, and (if the history is any guide) finally the dead chupawannabe will be revealed as a diseased canid. Perhaps one day an actual unknown mystery beast will be captured dead or alive, but until then there's more than enough speculation, folklore, and myth to keep the belief alive.

6

The Curious Case
of the Cuero Chupacabra

For years, Phylis Canion, a rancher outside the small Texas town of
Cuero, had dealt with animals occasionally preying on her household cats
and small livestock. In July 2007 she would finally find out what was attacking her animals—and it would change the course of her life. She would soon
become the world's most famous chupacabra owner, and proudly adopt the
mantle of "Chupacabra Lady."

I investigated Canion's chupacabra in April 2008 for the Discovery
Channel TV show *Monsterquest*. I flew to San Antonio, where I met with the
producer, a friendly if harried guy named Joe. He asked me about the chupacabra. I explained that I had already interviewed Phylis, and that based on
the history of chupacabra sightings (and claimed recoveries; see last chapter),
I suspected she simply had a coyote or feral dog with mange. I was, however,
open to the possibility of a real chupacabra, and eager to see it.

We headed out early the next morning for the hour-long drive. As we
drove away from the congestion of San Antonio, the land flattened out and
the houses got farther and farther apart. Ranches replaced town homes and
barbeque restaurants along the asphalt strip, and finally we pulled up in front
of Canion's ranch. Phylis—a short sparkplug of a woman sporting a shock of
blonde hair popping out above a red visor—came down off her porch and
greeted us warmly. TV crew in tow, we were invited to her home. Amid many
mounted animals attesting to her interest in wildlife, she told us her story.

Although some predation is common on ranches, in July 2007 the attacks
on her animals took a bolder and more mysterious turn. A few times she had

Figure 30. Phylis Canion shows a television crew where in 2007 she found a chupacabra near her ranch in Cuero, Texas. Photo by the author.

seen a bluish-gray, hairless animal (three of them, as it would turn out) lurking around her ranch, and suspected them of killing more than two dozen chickens over the previous few years. Canion said, "I had chickens, and not long after I had seen the first [animal], I came home and there was a chicken dead, but not carried off. It appeared to have all of the blood drained out of it" (2007a).

Canion said that whatever attacked her animals was no ordinary predator common to the area, such as a wild dog, bobcat, fox, or coyote: "Any predator we have here would normally carry the game off . . . a coyote would carry the chicken off." Eventually Canion decided to make it her mission to capture the strange-looking animal, either alive or on videotape. "I set up a video camera and started filming where the chickens were," she told me. After weeks and months, the mysterious creature remained elusive. "I have a gazillion feet of film that shows coyote coming up and taking the chicken, and a wild dog, and a bobcat, but never got this thing on film" (Canion 2008).

Animals disappeared now and then, but nothing definitive was found until July 14, 2007, when Phylis got a call telling her a strange animal had been found lying on the road: "The rancher behind me called me on a Saturday morning and said I should go look at this thing, I think it's what's been killing the chickens." Phylis immediately drove over to meet the rancher and see what he had found. Sure enough it was a bizarre, hairless four-legged creature. But there was an even bigger surprise to come. While she stood over the mysterious animal trying to make sense of it, her neighbor got a cell phone call saying that a second animal had just been found—in front of Phylis's own house!

She remembers staring down at the thing in disbelief. "I've been tracking this thing for two and a half years, and now within an hour we have two of them? I don't think so, it's probably a dog," she said. Still, she got in her vehicle and drove back toward her house to see what had been found. "Lo and behold, right there on the center stripe is this beast laying there. I went back to the house and called my sister and brother, and they said, 'Go pick it up!' And so I went with the tractor and got a bucket and brought it back to the house and laid it on the feed sack that you see it on in the pictures" (fig. 31).

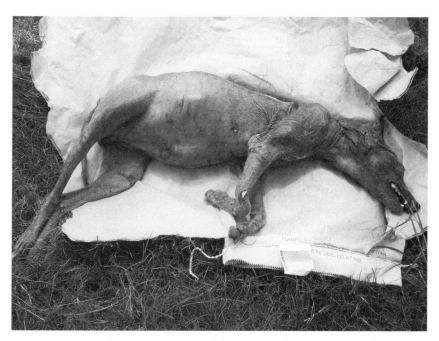

Figure 31. The famous chupacabra found by Phylis Canion near her ranch outside Cuero, Texas, in 2007. Photo courtesy of Phylis Canion.

She photographed the carcass, and the animal was unlike any she had ever seen. It had large ears, large fanged teeth, with grayish-blue elephantine skin. "I've seen a lot of nasty stuff. I've never seen anything like this," she said. "What makes this animal so unusual is that it has very large canine teeth [and] no indications of teeth on the top or bottom. I'm no mammalogist, but other animals have teeth all the way around." Adding to the puzzle, Canion said the creature was "completely hairless" (Canion 2007c, 2007d).

The Chupacabra

I asked to examine the chupacabra, and Phylis was happy to oblige. She led me into a side room and opened a freezer door. What emerged in her gloved hand was creepy: a severed head in a bag. (I did not grow up in a hunting family, so perhaps others would be less surprised to see an animal's head bagged in a freezer, but it certainly gave me chills.) I could smell the pungent, gamey stench of ripped flesh before I could see it. The cold had slowed the decay, but done little to dampen the smell. She placed the head in a sink, and began unwrapping it from the plastic trash bag. As she unwrapped each layer of plastic, my anticipation and excitement increased. I caught myself holding my breath.

After years of researching (and searching for) the chupacabra, I finally had a specimen in front of me. Others had escaped after giving only tantalizing glimpses, but finally here it was. Whether or not it was *the* chupacabra (the bloodthirsty beast of legend come alive, however briefly), it was certainly *a* chupacabra (claimed to be the creature)—and the most famous one in the world at that.

Phylis pulled the dead head out and I stared at it intently, as if it might open its eyes and tell me its strange story. It looked like something Death himself would have brought with him in his suitcase: dark gray, moist leathery skin and cream-colored fangs. Just as Madelyne Tolentino's 1995 eyewitness description of her encounter finally put an ugly face on the Puerto Rican goatsucker, Canion's beast gave the American chupacabra a definitive face and form (and funk). But was it *really* the long-sought chupacabra? The head, in all its gruesome glory, was intriguing, but it did not come with a consumer label on it declaring contents to be 100 percent chupacabra, *hecho en Puerto Rico*. It looked a lot like a dog or coyote to me—a nasty, slimy, diseased one that had definitely seen better days—but a canid nonetheless.

Obviously the best proof of its chupacabric nature would be a videotape of this beast sucking the blood out of chickens and goats; failing that, the next

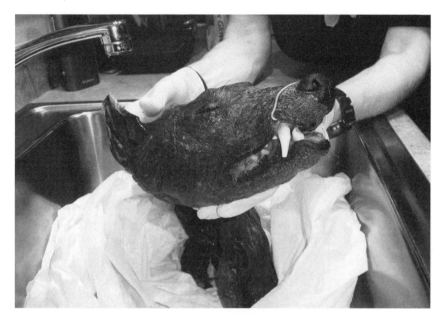

Figure 32. The severed head of the Cuero chupacabra. Photo by the author.

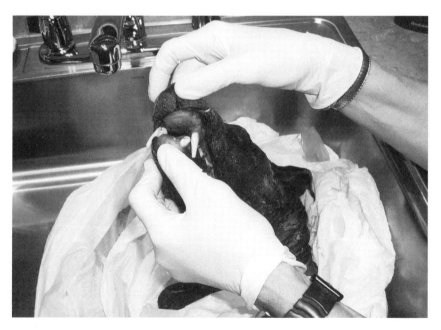

Figure 33. Terrifying teeth of the Cuero chupacabra. Photo by the author.

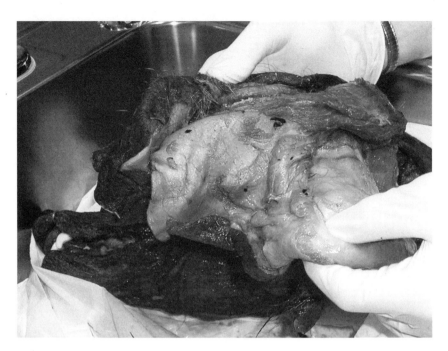

Figure 34. The Cuero chupacabra's neck and torso flesh. Photo by the author.

best thing would have to come later with the slowness (and sureness) of science in the form of DNA analysis. In fact, a local TV station had done just that. Samples of the monster's skin and muscle tissue were sent to a biologist at a university for DNA analysis, paid for by San Antonio television station KENS. The testing was done by Michael Forstner, PhD, a professor in the Department of Biology at Texas State University–San Marcos. Forstner's lab normally does DNA testing on a large number of different kinds of animals. In fact, Forstner's research had discovered several new animals—nothing potentially mythical, but "things that are typically cryptic, small, and they exist in places like 140 feet off the forest floor in Ecuador" (Forstner 2009).

Chupawhat?

When Phylis first found the carcass, many people accepted her conclusion that she had in fact found the chupacabra. After all, they said, it sucked the blood from livestock and it was weird looking; what else could it be? Journalists and the news media, to no one's surprise, were far more interested in the mystery-mongering angle to the story than in any skepticism; however, a few experts were duly quoted expressing some doubts about the animal. Travis Schaar, a veterinarian in the nearby town of Victoria, examined the chupacabra and suggested a more ordinary explanation: "I'm not going to tell you that it's not a chupacabra. I just think in my opinion a chupacabra is a dog," Schaar told the Associated Press (White 2007). Others suggested the animal might be a coyote.

After examining the head at length, I asked Phylis why she was so convinced it could not be a mangy coyote or dog. "Living on a ranch, we've seen a lot of different animals, including mangy coyotes," she told me. "When I first saw this, I was pretty convinced it was not a mangy coyote because it had no hair on it at all. And if you're familiar with coyotes, even if they have sarcoptic mange, they still have patches of hair. It had no hair, and short front legs." No, she said. The lack of hair clinched it for her: this was no coyote.

I asked Canion about the suggestion that the animal might be a Xolo dog (which as we have seen had been suspected in previous cases). "The closest Xolo dog is eighty miles away, and there has never been a history of that animal being loose," she replied. (Her confidence in her opinions aside, it's not clear why she would assume that she would know if there was a Xolo dog anywhere in the area, and of course just because she had not heard of any recent sightings does not mean that no one else has seen them.)

As Canion and the world waited for the DNA results, the news media got wind of the story. As word of Canion's discovery spread, the Cuero chupacabra became a media sensation. It made international news; television crews from as far away as Japan and Italy arrived to see Canion and her chupacabra. She sold thousands of "2007: Summer of the Chupacabra" T-shirts and caps. She got hundreds of letters from people around the world, from journalists to amateur monster hunters to schoolchildren. She had finally captured an animal she had been seeking for years, and it turned her life around.

The DNA Results

The scientific testing was finally done, and San Antonio reporter Joe Conger hosted a "special live television event" on Halloween night (Conger 2007a, 2007b). Ads for the special teased, "Scientific proof that the chupacabra is real? The KENS-5 I-Team reveals the exclusive DNA results of a creature that has the nation talking." Prof. Forstner and Phylis Canion were brought on camera for the moment of truth as Conger dramatically opened a folded page and read the results. This was the Academy Awards moment of cryptozoology. The animal was . . . a coyote.

"The DNA sequence is a virtually identical match to DNA from the coyote," Forstner said. "I really thought it was a domestic dog, but the Cuero chupacabra is a Texas coyote." Canion, clearly surprised and unhappy with the results, challenged Forstner to explain why the animal didn't look like a coyote, and he replied that it probably had mange.

I asked Forstner about his genetic analysis of the Cuero chupacabra. "In this case we had the material . . . I mean, it's a vertebrate. It's not going to be hard to match this, there are markers for mitochondrial DNA that are easy enough to match against almost any vertebrate on the planet, and those are available on GenBank. So we went to work and indeed that's pretty much where we ended up" (Forstner 2009).

At first, Forstner's concern was that Canion had found someone's beloved pet (perhaps from the Addams family?). "The sequencing immediately went to the family Canidae, and our immediate concern was that this was going to turn out to be somebody's pet dog. . . . Dogs in general, despite having great phenotypic variation—they all look different—are all pretty much the same genetically. So it was already going to be an issue, if it turned out to be a dog, *which* dog it was."

Soon, however, it became clear that the sample contained a marker that positively identified it as coyote: "We got the sequences back, uniquely within coyote there's an area of the D-loop, which is the area of mitochondrial DNA . . . it gives us data on things that are closely related . . . Uniquely in coyotes there's a deletion of several bases in one section, and another deletion in another area of an additional seven-base block. Turns out that the sequences that came back had those two unique deletions, and did not match any dogs or wolf. It came back with 97% confidence that it was *Canis latrans*, which is the coyote."

Prof. Forstner agreed to do the tests to help the public understand how science answers questions. "This is fun, not scary, but if people are worried about the chupacabra, it is probably even more important that we explain the mystery," he said. "Folks can fear what they don't understand, and a big part of the goal in science is to explain the natural world."

Disputing DNA

Perhaps not surprisingly, (and like previous chupacabra carcass owners), Canion was not happy with the DNA results and disputed the scientists' conclusion. "I'm like, No. I do not believe that it is coyote. It's got some kind of canine in it, but it is not all coyote. . . . I asked for DNA, and I looked at it. I am a naturopathic doctor and I practice with a group of doctors, and we all looked at the DNA and unanimously agreed that there was no way it was close to being an exact match," Canion said in an interview with the Paranormal Café podcast (2007b). While it certainly is true that DNA testing is not perfect, there was little scientific basis to question the test's validity. Canion convinced herself (and others) that the test was flawed, but naturopathic doctors have no training in DNA sequencing or analysis. Canion is certainly entitled to her opinion, but she is no more qualified to interpret the DNA results than is an airline pilot or an accountant. Even many medical doctors with years of training do not necessarily have the scientific expertise to interpret DNA results.[1]

A few others were also skeptical of the results. On an Internet forum set up to discuss the results (Forstner 2007a and 2007b), a man named Jim Jackson challenged Forstner: "The 'revelation' that DNA sequencing proved the Cuero animal was a coyote was flawed. The DNA used for sequencing was mitochondrial, which is inherited from the maternal lineage. Thus, one cannot rule out the Cuero animal had a chupacabra for a father, and was, indeed, half-chupacabra."

Forstner responded, "Actually, the way to look at the one-gene answer is that extraordinary claims require extraordinary evidence. I can accept that we only know the maternal lineage, but the logic inherent in contradicting the results with the single marker argument is itself flawed, as it presupposes the alternative (hybrid or other) hypothesis is more likely to explain the evidence. Effectively, to promote a hybrid or other origin is certainly a viable statement, just, do we really require exhaustive treatment of the topic to have an answer? I would argue that we have a ten to fifteen kilogram canid from south Texas with mitochondrial DNA of coyote, the skull age places it as a senior animal, and that seems like a pretty safe decision from the standpoint of what we know about mammals and wildlife in Texas."

The suggestion that the beast's father might be a chupacabra is theoretically possible, but there is no evidence for such a claim. Using that logic, one could make an equally valid argument that the animal's father could have been a dragon, a unicorn, or a Bigfoot. Wild speculation is fine, but brings us no closer to the truth. If all the evidence points to a coyote, it's probably a coyote.

In fact, soon a second DNA test confirmed this answer. Canion sought a second opinion, and spent $1,000 to have another sample of the beast analyzed at a genetics lab at the University of California at Davis. A few weeks later, Canion heard back. The results were virtually identical to those released by the University of Texas, but with a slightly more specific twist. "They said it is coyote on the maternal side only, and Mexican Wolf on the paternal side," she told me. Though Canion had vehemently disagreed with the results of the first test, she readily accepted the second.

I asked Prof. Forstner what he made of the second set of DNA tests. He said that while he had not spoken with the scientists at UC Davis, "my guess is that she didn't accept their first answer any better than she did mine, and to mollify her they said, 'Well this allele does occur in Mexican Wolves.' But that occurrence doesn't mean that it has any Mexican Wolf in it, or that it's somehow related. It means that we don't fully understand the genetics of coyotes in Texas and what that relationship to the database of existing alleles for captive Mexican Wolves is. It doesn't change the fundamental outcome, which is this is a coyote" (Forstner 2009).

Canid Soup: Coyotes, Dogs, and Chupacabras

Michael Bowdenchuck, state director for the Texas Wildlife Services program, said his department had been asked to provide DNA evidence to a California lab looking into the chupacabra. He cautions that finding that some coyotes, including Canion's specimen, might contain a significant trace of wolf DNA is interesting, but hardly unexpected. Since coyotes and wolves (and dogs, for that matter) belong to the same biological family, *Canidae*, they are closely related, and interbreeding between the species is not uncommon. "When you get into DNA of coyotes and canines, it really becomes something of a soup because we now have the ability to test for things we can't understand. You know, they're saying 'Well, there's wolf DNA, or red wolf DNA,' when in fact we're going back so many thousands of years to when that might have occurred, that maybe red wolves and coyotes weren't that different back then" (Bowdenchuck 2010). If you understand the science behind genetics, you realize that finding an allele that occurs in Mexican Wolves in a coyote is hardly surprising, though finding the same allele in a hummingbird might be very mysterious.

Derek Quann, resource conservation manager for Canada's Cape Breton Highland National Park, agrees: "It's pretty well accepted that coyotes are wolf hybrids," he said (quoted in Royte 2010). The fact that Canid genetics are not completely understood should not surprise anyone, nor does it suggest anything mysterious. *Outside* writer Elizabeth Royte notes that the science is very new: "It's only within the past three years—as monitoring technology has improved and the price of genetic analysis (of scat, hair, and hide from museum specimens) has dropped—that scientists have proved definitively that wolves and coyotes have interbred . . . Many are left wondering whether the resulting combination of traits, both behavioral and physiological, could be a recipe for future attacks" (Royte 2010).

In the end, Phylis Canion acknowledges that she has a coyote. But she also insists that she has the chupacabra. That is, she is convinced that chupacabras *are* coyotes with some mix of wolf hybrid. With everyone agreeing that the Cuero chupacabra is all or mostly coyote, other questions remain. Why was it hairless? Why did it suck the blood from her animals, if indeed it did? And why is her chupacabra completely different from the Puerto Rican version of the monster?[2]

Disguising Coyotes

The most obvious reason for the animal's lack of hair is the skin disease mange, though Phylis doesn't think the animal had mange. Mange is a parasitic infection caused by mites. Animals afflicted with mange often look strange, either hairless or partly hairless. Sarcoptic mange, a highly contagious form of the disease, can cause hair loss as well as extensive skin welts and crusting. Because people usually see animals with their full coat of fur, animals with mange can be difficult to identify. Canion believes the animal did not have mange because she did not see any mites or sores: "There were not sore spots on it; usually when you see sarcoptic mange in an animal they rub and rub until it becomes raw, and that did not happen on this animal." Besides that, she insists, the animal was completely bald, which would be very unusual even for an animal with mange, since usually there are at least some patches of hair.

Experts, however, disagree. Professor Forstner notes that "mange in coyotes in its most severe form typically leaves a line of fur at the ruff, behind the ears, and down the back." In fact, a close review of the original photographs that Canion took on July 14, 2007, clearly shows a significant line of fur stretching back along the neck and spine behind the ears of the animal—a signature characteristic of sarcoptic mange. By the time I examined and photographed the beast's head, much of the hair had fallen out (likely due to the carcass's being frozen, handled, thawed, bleached, and so on). Yet a close look at my photos reveals several patches of long hair on the animal even a year later (see fig. 34).

While it may be true that the animal had very little hair, Phylis Canion's assertion that there was no hair on the animal at all (a claim she repeated many times) is simply not true; photographs prove her wrong. The difference between "no hair at all" and visible patches of hair on the beast is not (pardon the pun) an exercise in splitting hairs; it is actually a very important distinction, because the complete lack of hair was a big part of the reason Canion concluded it could not be a mangy coyote. If it was truly and completely hairless, that would be remarkable, but if it was just *mostly* hairless (which it was), then it was almost certainly an advanced stage of mange (whether Canion agrees with the diagnosis or not). Canion, though a hunter and rancher, is not necessarily an expert on animal predation, nor infectious canid skin diseases. Just because the coyote had more mange on it than others Canion had seen does not mean it is a different animal.

There are other reasons why Canion might not have recognized the coyote. In addition to mange, feral animals may have other associated health problems, wounds, and diseases that help to create an unnatural appearance. A juvenile coyote, for example, whose growth has been stunted by a lack of food might appear about the size of a small dog, yet not share the distinctive features of a dog. The fact that the coyote was in poor health would also explain the tooth loss that Canion noted. Canion mentioned several characteristics about her animal that she found to be strange or mysterious. For example, she said, "One of the vets I showed it to said it did not necessarily have the body of a coyote because of the size of the belly." While the animal did not have all of the typical characteristics of a coyote, there is of course natural variation within a species. Just as not all dogs or people look the same, not all coyotes will either; some will have different color hair patterns, be fatter or thinner, and so on.

Just because Canion's chupacoyote did not match her idea (or her veterinarian friend's idea) of what a coyote should look like does not mean it is not a coyote; it just means that there is more variation in coyote morphology than these two nonexperts realize.

Vampire Claims

Even though most of Canion's assumptions about dogs and coyotes are shown to be mistaken, even if identifying mange and coyote behavior and morphology are beyond her expertise, the bloodsucking mystery remains. Canion is certain that the dead animals she'd seen had encountered a vampire. "There was never a doubt in my mind that there was no blood left in those animals,"

Canion told me. Yet, as we saw with the issue of the hair photographed on the "completely hairless" animal, Canion has shown herself to be a less than careful observer. Just because she did not see any blood around the dead animals does not prove they were drained of blood. Unless she actually took the animals for an autopsy there is no way for Canion to be sure there was no blood in the animals. Canion never had a professional necropsy done that would conclusively prove they had been drained of blood.

Though two puncture wounds on the neck could easily kill an animal through shock, suffocation, or a broken neck, an animal won't "bleed out" through two small holes. If a person is expecting to see pools of blood around a dead animal, but such pools are absent, the absence of blood could easily—and completely incorrectly—be mistaken for blood loss. Forstner doubts that Canion's claims of the animal bloodsucking are accurate. "I don't believe we have any empirical evidence that suggests we have animals sucking blood. That's something that needs to be substantiated." For a complete examination of the vampirism claims about this and other chupacabras, see chapter 8, "The Zoology of Chupacabras and the Science of Vampires."

Chupacabra Variation

If Phylis Canion has indeed finally found the dreaded chupacabra, she still must explain why her creature looks so different from many of the eyewitness reports. As I handled (and smelled) the chupacabra head at Canion's ranch, I couldn't help thinking back to Madelyne Tolentino's 1995 sighting. This animal was completely different from the creature Tolentino described.

I asked Canion why she thought that her chupacabra differed so dramatically from the Puerto Rican chupacabra. She said, "The pictures that we see show them standing upright, hence the short front legs. It shows them with red eyes. This creature has blue eyes. Well, what happens with blue eyes? When you take a picture they reflect red. So it's like, 'Okay, that now makes sense.' So what about the spines down the back? When you look at some of the pictures [drawings] of the chupacabra it's got spines down its back. And based on what all three of these looked like from behind the ears to six inches back, they had very long hair. Only a little strip, like a hyena. And . . . those three things, the blue eyes, the short legs, and the hair down the back, is what evolved from what pictures were from a hundred years ago of the chupacabra."

In an interview on the Paranormal Café podcast, Canion elaborated on her belief that the chupacabra had blue eyes, and speculated on the reasons why it has been reported to have glowing red eyes. "I have blue eyes, and when people take pictures of people with blue eyes, they always have to use red eye reduction because the eyes show up so red. So when these old pictures of the chupacabra where they have the red eyes, could it be because this animal has blue eyes, that it has such a red reflection?" (Canion 2007b). This idea apparently made perfect sense to Paranormal Café host Rob Simcox, who responded, "That's a good point, I hadn't thought of that . . . being that the eye is so pale, it can't absorb the light and reflects it back."

Canion deserves credit for making an attempt to reconcile the different chupacabra descriptions with her own carcass. But her argument fails immediately when you consider that the glowing red eyes she is referring to did *not* appear in photographs at all. Instead, the creepy red eyes were allegedly seen *in person*; there was no camera flash that could have possibly created the red-eye effect in the first place. And there were certainly no photographs of the beast's red eyes "from a hundred years ago," since the chupacabra only dates back to 1995. Furthermore, the "red eye" camera effect occurs with eyes of *all* colors and certainly doesn't only appear in photographs of blue-eyed people. Canion also contradicts herself regarding the animal's being hairless, insisting repeatedly that it did not have hair, then acknowledging a significant amount of hair in a mange-like strip down the back that might be mistaken for spikes down the back.

Though Canion tries to bolster her claims by citing other chupacabra-related elements and phenomena, she actually fatally undermines the validity of her argument with a tangled and often self-contradictory mass of errors and mistakes.

Canion's Chupacoyote

Canion remains convinced that she has a chupacabra, an animal that is a hybrid or crossbreed of Mexican wolf and coyote. There are several serious problems with this "explanation," which raises more questions than it answers. For example, it does not explain why or how a cross between two animals (neither of which drink blood) would somehow create an animal with essentially coyote-like characteristics but whose body and digestive system have presumably somehow adapted from eating small animals to drinking blood for sustenance (for more on this, see chapter 8).

There's another fatal flaw in Canion's argument. Scientists and wildlife experts already *know* what coyote/wolf hybrids look like; they have been studied for years. These "coywolves" do not suck blood, nor do they have any of the chupacabra's unique characteristics. In fact, many scientists regard the American Red Wolf (*Canis rufus*) as a coyote/wolf hybrid based on its DNA composition. Professor Forstner told me that "[i]n the eastern U.S. Red Wolf, they have been argued over time and in the scientific literature to simply be a hybrid of coyote and wolf. Or to be a unique strain that was isolated in the East that was a forest-dwelling wolf/coyote animal. The same argument has been made about the captive Mexican Wolf, and was contaminated by coyotes early on by animals that were not pure strains" (Forstner 2009). Ironically, if Canion is correct in her belief about the chupacabra's genetic makeup, hers is only one of many known "chupacabra" specimens that have been studied for decades by mainstream zoologists.

Labeling the Chupacabra

I asked Canion who first identified the beast as the chupacabra. "My brother," she said. "He was the first one I called, and I said, 'I don't know what it is, but it's sucking the blood out of my chickens.' He said, 'Oh, that's the chupacabra . . . the blood sucker.' I said, 'Get out of here! How do you know about that?' He said some of the Hispanics that work on our ranch, they always talk about *el chupacabra*."

Thus the connection to Hispanic culture and folklore becomes clear. It was not Phylis Canion who independently assumed that the predation was necessarily the work of the Hispanic goatsucker, but her Spanish-speaking ranch hands. In a classic example of how different chupacabra accounts, reports, and eyewitnesses influence and seemingly reinforce each other's validity, Canion "confirmed" her chupacabra by looking at images on the Internet. "I was telling my brother, I saw this weird thing on the ranch that didn't have any hair on it, short front legs and all, and he said, 'That's the chupacabra.' I said, 'How do you know?' and he said, 'Get on the Internet, look for chupacabra and look at the pictures.' So I did, and it looked like the one killed in Elmendorf." (This actually does not support the credibility of her animal, since the Elmendorf Beast turned out to be a dog; see chapter 5.)

Canion said, "Everyone kept telling me that's exactly what it is, if the blood is drained." That is, if Canion is correct that her chickens were drained of blood, then the most likely explanation (at least among several people in her area) is that it must be the work of the chupacabra—what else would it be?

This is what is known in formal logic as a conditional argument. *If* X is true, *then* Y is true: *If* the animals were drained of blood, *then* it must have been done by the chupacabra. (This is not necessarily valid, since there may be other reasons an animal could possibly be drained of blood, but for the sake of argument let's say it is true.) There is no good evidence that the chickens were in fact drained of blood; if they were not, then there is no reason to suspect anything odd or unusual attacked them. That is, to conclude that the chupacabra attacked the dead animals, we must first prove that the animals were victims of a vampire.

In the case of the Cuero chupacabra and others, there were two apparently unusual incidents that occurred. Canion had endured apparently odd blood-drained predation (mystery number 1), and later found a strange animal (mystery number 2). Taken individually, neither event is especially mysterious, but when combined they seem to complement each other, and help solve each other's mystery. This is a logical fallacy with the fancy Latin name of *post hoc ergo propter hoc*, which means "after this, therefore because of it." It is a common mistake, where we assume that just because event B happened *after* event A, event A *caused* event B. In the case of the Cuero chupa, both mysteries are solved, and neither can be logically used to support the other. There is no good evidence that any of Canion's animals were drained of blood, and the best evidence is that the animal she found is a coyote.

Remember also that despite Canion's sustained efforts at videotaping the chupacabra (resulting in "a gazillion feet of film"), the only animals seen were ordinary, natural predators. If the chupacabras were actually attacking her livestock, it seems likely they would have been caught on camera. In short, every predator seen attacking the animals on Canion's ranch was a normal, typical one—and not a single unknown or mystery beast was filmed.

All the evidence taken together points to one inescapable conclusion: the Cuero chupacabra is exactly what both DNA tests say it is: a sickly coyote in the advanced stages of mange that may or may not have attacked animals but could not have sucked their blood.

Why does Canion continue to insist that she has a chupacabra, despite so much evidence and so many arguments to the contrary? Mike Forstner believes that Canion has too much invested in her role as "The Chupacabra Lady" to accept that she simply has a mangy coyote. To accept that hers is an ordinary animal is to lose face and risk embarrassment. "Phylis Canion told me she was making $8,000 a month on T-shirts. And she had publicly gone on TV and in the newspaper and to the people she lives and works with every day and said, 'I have this unique thing.' . . . From her perspective, it's 'It can't be something common because I don't think it's something common'" (Forstner 2009).

Indeed, the mystery animal—chupacabra or not—was a cash cow. Lakes containing alleged monsters sell tourist memorabilia; Bigfoot tourism makes a lot of money for some folks in the Pacific Northwest; and the potential to cash in on her chupacabra was not lost on Phylis Canion. Her website, Chupacabra Central (at cuerochupacabra.com), offers plenty of gear for the monster enthusiast. A two-tone, 14-karat gold and sterling silver chupacabra charm is available for $35 and up; she also has a variety of T-shirts, hats, beer coolers, polo shirts, and an aluminum "Beware: Chupacabra Crossing" sign, so that motorists will be sure not to kill the animals on the road (though ironically that's how Canion obtained her chupacabra; perhaps she wants to discourage competition).

I asked Professor Forstner what he made of his role in solving the mystery of the world's most famous chupacabra. "It's like finding out what Rodney Dangerfield meant . . . [about getting no respect]. I've had twenty years of success in conservation genetics and I get more attention having done an ad hoc coyote sequence than I have almost in any other quality work that we have done on any endangered species that was really hard to do." Still, Forstner sees some positive aspects to the case. "There's been a real benefit. My students have learned more about how pop science works, and about how science interfaces with the public from this, than almost anything else we do." Furthermore, despite debunking the Cuero animal, he gained experience and information that may actually help identify future chupacabras (or would-be chupacabras). He routinely receives photographs of mangy coyotes from people all over central Texas. "I am now the Official Coyote Mange Photo Recipient," Forstner told me drily. "As a result, we now have many images of coyotes with mange that mimic the images that Phylis has. We have gotten more valuable information about coyotes, mange, and the occurrence in Texas than we had before."

Conclusion

Every single recovered alleged chupacabra that has been tested has been scientifically identified. Whether a dog, skate, coyote, or another animal, science eventually found an answer. In some cases, the animal bore little or no real relation to any "true" chupacabra—whether or not any of them could *possibly* be a chupacabra specimen, the important issue is that at some point they were *identified* as a chupacabra.

As I noted in the first chapter, one of the distinguishing characteristics of the chupacabra is the wide variety of forms it takes. No one knows for sure what the chupacabra looks like—or, more correctly, dozens of people "know" what it looks like, and rarely do any two descriptions fully agree. There is no gold standard, no type specimen to compare reports to. The only thing that all reported chupacabras have in common is that someone identified them as a chupacabra—the identification itself (across an impossibly wide variety of descriptions) is key to its nature.

Though *chupacabra* literally means "goatsucker," figuratively it means "scapegoat"—something that is blamed for some unrelated consequence of another cause. When ranchers (particularly those who speak Spanish, or are Hispanic) don't know or can't explain what's attacking their livestock, they often conclude that it must be a chupacabra. This, however, is a logical fallacy called arguing from ignorance. It's basically taking a lack of evidence or knowledge about something ("We don't know what's doing this") and drawing a conclusion from that lack information ("therefore it must be a chupacabra"). But the chupacabra label does not follow. Just because a rancher or farmer can't explain how a chicken or goat or cow died doesn't mean it's mysterious, or that someone else can't explain it. And it certainly doesn't mean that the animal is a victim of the chupacabra.

In fact, "chupacabra" is not an explanation for anything; it is not an answer. Calling something a chupacabra is simply answering a riddle with another riddle. We have something that appears strange and mysterious (attacks, mutilations), and don't have an obvious answer; therefore we create the chupacabra.

Those who find the dead animals—the alleged chupacabra victims—are never forensic or medical experts; instead they are farmers and ranch hands. They may be very knowledgeable about agriculture, ranching, or animal husbandry, but are out of their element when coming to conclusions about what killed dead animals. The question of what killed an animal is, after all, ultimately a medical and forensic question. In the next chapter we see what light modern forensic investigation can shed on the mystery.

PART IV

SOLVING THE MYSTERY
OF THE CHUPACABRA

7

Reconsidering the Goatsucker

So far we have examined the chupacabra mystery from a variety of perspectives: as a product of folklore, from eyewitness accounts, as animal carcasses found in a half-dozen states and countries, and so on. Many of the questions surrounding the chupacabra have been answered, though a few mysteries remain.

One of the biggest unanswered questions about the beast is where the chupacabra came from. Whether a real animal, a cultural meme or legend, or some combination of them, the goatsucker must have an origin, some root or thread that we can follow, leading us to a satisfying starting point.

A second unanswered question is what eyewitnesses are reporting when they claim to have encountered the chupacabra. A known or unknown animal? A phantom vampire? A figment of the imagination? As it turns out, these two questions are closely linked.

This is the point in the analysis in which most authors leave the subject, wrap up the book, proclaim that some mysteries will never be solved, and move on. But to answer the questions, to really understand the phenomenon and solve the fifteen-year-old mystery of the goatsucker, we must dig deeper. We must take a closer look at the evidence and reconsider the chupacabra.

Eyewitness Reports

Why did eyewitnesses report seeing the chupacabra in so many different forms? The obvious answer is the correct one: the descriptions are different because the eyewitnesses saw different things. Few of them—in fact perhaps none of them—saw anything that had actually attacked animals, much less sucked their blood. One might have been startled by a bat or an owl; another a leaping dog; perhaps another saw a burglar lurking in shadows. Still others may have made up their sightings for fun or attention.[1] Since the sightings invariably offered little in the way of evidence, one report was about as good as the next, and even the most outlandish stories were more or less accepted and reported uncritically. Their only common link was that they occurred when stories of this mysterious chupacabra beast were circulating in the rumor mills, in bars, and on television and in the newspapers.

As chupacabra researcher Jon Downes told me, "All the eyewitnesses are perceptually clouded by their own cultural preconceptions. I have met a few out-and-out hoaxers who are only in it for the money, and a number of people who are clearly mad . . . I haven't read one eyewitness report yet that is conclusive, and the eyewitnesses I have met who claim to have seen a chupacabra crouching over the victim lapping its blood have been the least credible, and the most bonkers" (Downes 2009).

Furthermore, Downes noted, the original chupacabra description, Tolentino's detailed beast—was actually confined more or less to one specific area, and the eyewitness reports became wilder and less credible (if such a phrase can be used) the more time elapsed and the more widespread the reports became. "The chupacabra—the spike-backed creature—has been seen only in these high grassland plateaus of Puerto Rico. The farther away you get from the Canovanas Plateau, the more stupid, the more sketchy, and the more unbelievable chupacabra reports become" (Downes 2009).

The Tolentino Eyewitness Report: A Closer Look

To solve a mystery you often need to understand where it came from, to seek out the original sighting that spawned the rest, the "case zero." As discussed in the first chapter, the best chupacabra sighting in history came from a woman named Madelyne Tolentino of Canovanas, Puerto Rico. It is the most important chupacabra description on record, not only because of its detail but also because it is the "original" chupacabra description upon which the most famous depictions of the creature are based. As Scott Corrales notes,

Figure 35. Madelyne Tolentino and her ex-husband, Miguel Agosto, at the spot where she sighted the chupacabra in 1995. Photo by the author.

"The first descriptions of this mysterious creature came about six months into the mutilation epidemic. In September, sightings by Madelyne Tolentino, a housewife of Canovanas—a city to the east of the island's capital, San Juan— and others gave it a form and a name" (Corrales 1996).

Most accounts of Tolentino's encounter offer only a brief summary of her description, but to really understand her account we must examine it in full. She claims to have seen the creature near her mother's house during the second week of August 1995 (she was unsure of the date). In an interview with members of the Puerto Rican Research Group in 1996 (published in Corrales 1997), Tolentino said the bipedal animal had dark gray or black eyes that "were damp and protruding, running up to its temples and spreading to the sides . . . [its height was] about four feet, more or less. At the time, it was walking like a human, on both legs. Its arms were drawn back in an 'attack position,' as though it were a TV monster . . . it has three, long, skinny fingers. The arms were also very long . . . [its hair] was rather short, and close to its body. Rather well-combed in fact . . . It had some round things on its body, and the region seemed ashen, as if something had burned it there. The burn mark revealed pinkish-purple skin, as if the top layer had fallen off." As for the creature's legs, Tolentino said, "they were very long and skinny, and I could see three separate toes . . . like a goose's foot, that has a little thing between its toes [presumably she means webbing] . . . for a nose, it had two little holes, and its mouth was a slash. It was closed. At no moment did it open its mouth, so I saw neither fangs nor teeth . . . I noticed something on its lower back. It looked like it had feathers . . . like feathers, but flat on its back. At no point did they rise. (In an interview conducted by Marc Davenport in February 1996, Madelyne said the 'feathers' became erect and moved rapidly from side to side). [The feathers] were joined by some sort of membrane, and it looked reddish, like a mixture of copper with brown and other colors."

Tolentino's curiosity about the chupacabra before her extended to its genitals: "I even got down on the floor to see if it had genitals. It had nothing at all—it was 'plain' and sealed. I laughed, and said to my mother, 'What the heck is this? Does it defecate through its mouth after it eats?' It made slow, robot-like

Figure 36. The street in Canovanas, Puerto Rico, where Madelyne Tolentino had the most famous chupacabra sighting in history. Photo by the author.

movements, as if being controlled by someone." At some point Tolentino screamed (it's not clear why), and "when my mother heard me scream, she decided to go out and grab the creature . . . The thing took off running . . . I noticed that it kind of hopped, like a kangaroo. It plunged into the woods [across from the house], my mother ran after it [and] a boy who works for my husband . . . went into the woods to catch the creature. He says that, when he tried to grab the creature, it whipped out what I thought were feathers. He says that they stood straight up and that they were very long spines. . . . The spines changed colors, and then he says he pried its mouth open and saw that it had really large fangs." According to Tolentino, the chupacabra broke free from the boy's impromptu dental inspection and "started running much faster than it had. Its feet weren't touching the ground. It was as if it had been suspended in the air, floating."

In 2010 I located and interviewed Tolentino in Puerto Rico (see appendix 3). She had more or less dropped out of sight for fifteen years, and she said I was the first journalist to interview her about her sighting since around 1995. The details and descriptions above reflect an interview shortly after her sighting (as translated and reprinted in Corrales 1997), and may be considered more reliable than her more recent recollections. Nonetheless, she made some interesting comments, and corrected many misunderstandings about her sighting. For example, she insisted that the widely seen drawing by Jorge Martín "based on her sighting" is inaccurate in several important ways. The creature she saw was much smaller than the four to five feet tall that Martín and others reported; instead Tolentino says it was only about three feet tall. Furthermore, it did not have three fingers but instead five; and those five fingers did not end in claws, as was widely reported, but instead looked quite human. "There were no claws," Tolentino stated categorically.[2]

Credibility Questions

Tolentino's story strains the credibility of even the most credulous readers (though, apparently, not of the Puerto Rican chupacabra researchers). Much in her incredibly detailed account is dubious, nonsensical, and contradictory. If Tolentino's account is accurate and truthful, the woman has near superhuman powers of observation; most witnesses would have only remembered a few of the most obvious features, but she spills out detail after detail of description, from its eye color to the number of toes on its feet to its missing anus. You would think she had gotten an up-close, 360-degree inspection, instead of seeing the creature from one vantage point (a window) at some distance in the early afternoon. Furthermore, if she was observing the chupacabra through a window, how could she have seen anything when she "got down on the floor" for a closer look at the creature's genitalia? She states that the creature "runs," but later says it "hopped," and finally concludes that it was neither running nor hopping but instead "floated." Which is it? Or did it run, then hop, then float? What, exactly are we to make of this?

Tolentino's description of what she and others did is hard to believe: after she sees this bizarre monster, she doesn't run or panic (or look for a camera), but instead she makes a joke about it with her mother, then inexplicably screams. Her mother then bravely chases this bizarre, otherworldly creature to try and catch it! She fails, but a local boy (his age is not given) manages to chase it into the woods, grab the monster, pry its mouth open, and then release it, all without injury? This is reported (and accepted) as fact, but the woman is simply reporting *what the boy later told her had occurred*, without any independent corroboration. It seems likely, if not almost certain, that the boy made up the story. (During her 2010 interview with me, Tolentino dismissed the boy's story as a lie or exaggeration.)

It is amazing that the Puerto Rican chupacabra researchers apparently didn't corroborate Tolentino's story with either her mother, the young boy, or another nearby man who first saw the creature. The members of the Puerto Rican Research Group apparently didn't conduct any sort of investigation at all, and instead merely interviewed Tolentino about her story. Reports of lost pets are treated with more professionalism and competence. This is not even amateur investigation, this is non-investigation, with little or no attempt made to determine the validity or truth of the report. Yet this account, clearly fabricated (or, at the very least, heavily embellished), is regularly presented as one of the best, most important pieces of evidence for the chupacabra.

Tolentino is not alone in her chupacabra-inspired creativity. Her then-husband, Miguel Agosto, described a struggle between a dog and a chupacabra he'd seen, soberly offering what must be one of the least believable details in chupacabra lore. He claims that "the creature had apparently shaved the place on the dog where it was going to make the incision." Even Agosto's interviewer, Lucy Plá, had a hard time believing that before the chupacabra drew blood from the dog, it had somehow gotten ahold of a razor and shaving cream (or visited a barbershop) and carefully shaved away the dog's fur from the area where it intended to suck the canine blood. "You're telling me that the creature cleans the spot where it's going to make the incision?" Plá asked.

"Precisely," responded Agosto (Corrales 1997, 57). He also later suggested that perhaps the chupacabra had ESP abilities, and telepathically controlled the mind of a police officer who had tried to shoot it. It seems clear that two of the most important chupacabra eyewitnesses have a fanciful imagination.

Even the least skeptical among us would have a hard time believing such fantastic tales. In many cases, the details and descriptions are contradictory. It may be that some details are accurate, while others are misunderstandings, embellishments, or outright fabrications. The problem is that even if one-third, half, or even most of what Tolentino reported is accurate, there's no way to know what is fact and what is fantasy, which details are true, which are speculation, and which are completely made up. If what Scott Corrales writes is accurate (and it may or may not be), Tolentino may have passed off misinformation as truth and fabricated details about the chupacabra.

Slippery Slime

Though there is no corroborating evidence of Tolentino's eyewitness claims, she did tell Puerto Rican researchers that during an attack on goats, the creature "leaves some sort of slime. It also left slime on some rabbits it killed [nearby]. The newspaperman from *El Vocero* kept it and sent it to Linda Moulton Howe, a lady from Pennsylvania . . . She had the slime analyzed over there, and says it's nothing from this world . . . They say they have no idea what it belongs to, but that it's nothing from this world" (Corrales 1997, 47).

Intrigued by Tolentino's report of otherworldly slime, I contacted Linda Moulton Howe and asked her for more information. I hoped that in the fifteen years since the samples were taken, something new had been discovered. What was the nature of the slime? Where was it analyzed, by whom, and what were the results? (And what qualities and characteristics, exactly, would lead a professional chemical analyst to conclude that the sample provided was "not of this world"?)

As often happens with tantalizing leads and promises of evidence in the realm of the chupacabra, Tolentino's story about the slime turned out to be a complete fabrication: no slime was found. Nor had any analysis been done on the nonexistent slime. Howe told me, "I spent two weeks in Puerto Rico in January 1996 investigating the chupacabra phenomenon there, but I never had any slime to analyze." Contradicting Tolentino's story, she said, "I don't know how some of these complete untruths get started" (Howe 2009).

Note that Tolentino's misinformation extended far beyond the slime's existence; she did not simply make a factual error, mistakenly believing that chupacabra slime had been found. Instead, the most famous and "credible" chupacabra eyewitness told a whole story about the slime: not only had it been found, but it had been scientifically analyzed; and that analysis proved that it was of extraterrestrial origin. As for Howe's question about how these stories get started, it seems that Tolentino and others embellished the story and so it stood for fifteen years, until I simply cross-checked her claim—basic research that previous chupacabra investigators and writers had failed to do. Tolentino offers second- and third-hand information—little more than rumors—as self-evident truth. The credibility of Tolentino and her husband has been seriously damaged, between the outlandish, illogical details and her statements that have been contradicted by others. On an important piece of information about the chupacabra, Tolentino was either lying or mistaken.[3]

There is no corroborating evidence of Tolentino's story, no physical proof or traces at all. All we have is her story. There is another, very persuasive reason to suspect that Tolentino's eyewitness account is not credible: about a half-dozen alleged chupacabra carcasses have been found (see chapters 5 and 6); almost all have a canid form; not a single one bears even a remote resemblance to the creature she described. There's a very good reason why the dead chupacabras don't match Tolentino's description: she almost certainly did not see what she reported seeing.

Tolentino's Influence

Tolentino's eyewitness account became the most detailed, important, and influential eyewitness report of the Puerto Rican chupacabra. About a month after her sighting, on September 12, she worked with a UFO researcher named Jorge Martín to develop a widely circulated drawing of the creature that Tolentino saw. The drawing (seen in figure 1) is a rough approximation of her description, though it contains many significant errors.[4] According to Tolentino, a much more accurate depiction of what she saw can be seen in figure 37A (though it was created before she revised details such as the shape and number of fingers). Martín's drawing was published on the front page of San Juan's *El Nuevo Día* newspaper, and as Scott Corrales (1997) noted, it "prompted the predator [chupacabra] into global notoriety and perhaps a permanent place in Puerto Rican myth." Indeed, "By November 1995, the now-famous portrait by the island's leading UFOlogist, Jorge Martín, had flashed around the world courtesy of the Internet" (Corrales 1996).

Perhaps more important, the drawing would become the "standard" depiction of the chupacabra; it put an assured face and corpus to a creature whose existence had, up until Tolentino's sighting, only been rumored. This drawing—this visual evidence based on a presumably sincere first-person eyewitness, published with authority on the front page of the newspaper— had a powerful effect on Puerto Ricans who believed in the creature and who had followed the news (or rumor mill) about the beast. It told the public what the chupacabra looked like, and therefore what to expect to see if they encountered it. In psychological terms, the public was primed to interpret any odd, mysterious, or unexpected encounters as chupacabra.

And that is exactly what happened. Consider the story of perhaps the third-most "credible" chupacabra eyewitness (after Madelyne Tolentino and her husband): Daniel Perez, a "serious and well-educated man . . . whose credibility was never an issue," who, according to Tolentino, saw a creature on a rock, and shouted to his wife, "'Brunhilda! A *chupacabras!*' He says the creature stood on the rock for a while, then suddenly leaped through two dense trees without damaging a single leaf."

It's hard to take such an "eyewitness" claim seriously as being factually accurate. Perez may or may not have seen some strange creature leap through trees, but unless he personally inspected each leaf and branch, there's no way he could truthfully and knowledgably make the statement that it leapt through two dense trees "without damaging a single leaf." This may seem like a minor point, but it is not. If this part of his eyewitness description is not literally true, what other parts are not literally true? What other parts of his story or description are embellished and hyperbole? Perhaps it didn't "leap" away but instead "flew" away—or did it "vanish"?

Perez's sighting was very influential in forming the public's idea of what the chupacabra looked like. Scott Corrales states that "Perez was not the only educated, perceptive member of the population who provided a highly detailed account . . . but his testimony was vital for an important reason. He was privileged to have seen the monster twice . . . The excellent drawing composed by Jorge Martín, which had been featured on the first page of San Juan's *El Nuevo Día* newspaper, was revised on the basis of the Perez testimony" (1997, 67).

Presumably the beast was not wearing an identifying name tag, so it's a fair question to ask how Perez immediately knew that the animal he was looking at was a chupacabra and not perhaps some other curious creature. The answer is that he—like every other witness following the publication of Martín's sketch on the front page of the local newspaper—was using Tolentino's original eyewitness report as a reference. "He had already seen the sketches," says Tolentino, "and already knew what it looked like" (Corrales 1997, 43). Tolentino's description of the creature she saw is clearly the most important and influential chupacabra depiction in history, literally the standard by which the credibility (and validity) of future reports were judged.

Because Tolentino's description is the original, "template" sighting, it set the rough parameters for future reports. If she had reported that the chupacabra had six legs and four eyes, it's likely that later eyewitnesses would have followed her lead and reported similar characteristics. It is important to remember that most alleged chupacabra sightings are in poor conditions, such as at dusk or at night; most are simply fleeting glimpses of *something* dark amid the shadows. Psychological studies have shown that under such conditions, the human mind is very poor at accurately perceiving, remembering, and reporting even basic elements of the experience. The human mind often "fills in" details with what we expect to see, and we tend to bias our reports accordingly. The same process can turn floating logs into lake monsters, brown bears into Bigfoot. This tendency is not news to psychologists or police detectives, but has strong relevance in this case.

Of course, just because Tolentino described her chupacabra in a specific way does not guarantee that others who report seeing the creature will automatically parrot her exact description. But there is a strong likelihood that their reports would be very similar, as widespread stress and panic make people more vulnerable to "groupthink," conformity, and social imitation (Janis 1963). As this relates to chupacabra reports, Robert Michael Jordan notes that "[t]hese conditions lead people to mimic the beliefs and behaviors of their neighbors and friends in order to maintain a collective identity and strengthen vital social bonds" (2008). Thus even if an eyewitness was sure he or she saw something thought to be the chupacabra but that was unlike Tolentino's description, that person would likely consciously or unconsciously change some details of the description to more closely match Tolentino's report so as not to discredit her.

This point brings us back to two of the greatest unsolved mysteries about the chupacabra. What, if anything, did Madelyne Tolentino see? Was Tolentino lying, telling tall tales, or did she actually see some creature? Where did she come up with the detailed description she gave Jorge Martín? Did she make up the details out of thin air, or is there another explanation? And why was the creature suddenly sighted in August 1995? Scott Corrales wrote that "it is almost certain that the creature's origin will never be clearly established" (2010), but it seems his pessimistic assessment was premature. As it turns out, one answer solves both mysteries. To understand why, we must return to the beginning.

Chupacabra: The Summer Blockbuster

Events, even strange ones—*especially* strange ones—don't occur in a vacuum. There are always some preexisting physical, psychological, or sociocultural conditions that set the stage. In early 1995, stories and rumors spread that some mysterious vampire was loose and had been preying on the island's animals, though the reports were sporadic, sensationalized, unconfirmed, and lacking any significant description of the mysterious beast. One curious question is why, in the midst of what one writer described as Puerto Ricans' "near-fever pitch" about the creature and the mutilations of "near-epidemic proportions across the island," the chupacabra was able to go about its bloody business attacking animals every few weeks for nearly half a year without being seen even once. Could it be that the chupacabra got sloppy with its disappearing act, and just happened to finally be sighted during the second week of August 1995?

Or perhaps something happened just before Tolentino's sighting—some new element had been added to the mix, something came to the island that had not existed there before—that could have spawned chupacabra sighting and given visage to the heretofore unseen creature.

The creature Tolentino described bears no resemblance to any known animal. It does, however, bear an uncanny similarity to a *fictional* creature seen by hundreds of thousands of people in 1995: Sil.

What *Species* is the Chupacabra?

Sil is the name of an alien creature played by Natasha Henstridge in the sci-fi horror film *Species*. The film's press kit summarizes the plot: "In 1974, the world's largest radio telescope relayed a message to the rest of the galaxy. Sponsored by the United States Government and drafted by a team of elite scientists, that message contained information about Earth and its inhabitants: what we looked like, where we were located, and most significantly, the DNA sequences that make up the human cell. Twenty years later, the inconceivable happened: the message was answered. Someone—or something—knows where to find us. The message contained a DNA sequence and the friendly instructions to combine it with our own. We believed we were in control; we presumed we could handle the result; we assumed we would always be dominant . . . We were wrong" (*Species* press kit 1995).

Species begins with a genetics experiment, led by scientist Xavier Fitch (played by Sir Ben Kingsley). He has injected the alien DNA sequence into human eggs; most died, but one was allowed to grow into a seemingly normal human child called Sil. But Fitch aborts the experiment when Sil begins aging at a fantastic rate, and during REM sleep, alien spikes emerge from the girl's spine. He reluctantly decides to kill Sil, fearing that the experiment may soon grow out of control—and it does. Sil escapes, and Fitch is forced to assemble an assassination team to track down the bizarre, humanoid creature before it wreaks havoc. The film, directed by Roger Donaldson and written by Dennis Feldman, was a massive box office success, earning over $113 million worldwide and spawning a series of successful sequels (the most recent was 2007's *Species: The Awakening*, set in Latin America).

The film itself is less interesting and important than its "star." Sil was designed by celebrated Swiss artist H. R. Giger. Known for his eerie, bizarre—and often erotic—art, Giger had previously worked with Hollywood filmmakers designing creatures in the *Alien* films. "When we thought about the creature, we felt that Giger was the only one who could give us what we wanted. We talked to him on the telephone, and found that he was intrigued by the idea of creating [Sil]," said *Species* producer Frank Mancuso Jr. (Shapiro 1995b). Just how similar is Giger's Sil alien to the Puerto Rican chupacabra?

Sil and the Chupacabra

The Sil alien and the creature that Tolentino described are remarkably similar. Both have large, red or black wraparound eyes; both have an elongated head; both have a tiny or nonexistent nose; both have five long fingers; both have a series of spikes along the spine; both have long, thin arms; both have long, thin legs; both are missing ears; both have a small, almost nonexistent mouth, and so on.

An internal February 9, 1994, memo from Metro-Goldwyn-Mayer producers Roger Donaldson and Frank Mancuso Jr. to H. R. Giger about the creature design provides a fascinating inside look at the ideas for Sil's nature, behavior, and physical description. It presages the later description of the Puerto Rican chupacabra so well that Jorge Martín's sketch of the creature could have come directly from the MGM studio production notes instead of from Madelyne Tolentino's memory (or imagination). Donaldson and Mancuso wrote, "In the monster form, Sil must be able to move easily and fast; She must have in her biology the means by which to kill without effort . . . We discussed the possibilities of things like bone spurs, tentacles, and/or a barbed, sharp tongue. . . . she should be able to burrow into the ground . . . she has extra-sensory ability" (Donaldson and Mancuso 1995). As for the creature's victims, "When Sil kills she should leave her victims dead in a very identifiable way. For example, if she broke or sucked all the bones [or blood] out of her victim, this would show that the body was killed by some extraordinary circumstances that could be used as a clue in deciding that this was no ordinary murder but that it was the work of our escaped alien. Sil should leave behind some evidence that she has been at a location . . . (i.e. bodily fluid, . . . odor, slime, gob, scratches, suction marks, etc.)."

Indeed, this is a near-verbatim list of physical characteristics claimed for the chupacabra (see chapter 1). The parallels are unmistakable, including the body shape, locomotion, burrowing ability, distinctive method of killing ("sucking" blood or internal organs), telepathic/ESP claims, leaving slime, distinctive odor, and so on. Furthermore, one characteristic that several Puerto Rican eyewitnesses—though not Tolentino herself—described was a long, snaking tongue. In the film, the creature (and her alien offspring) is seen with a long, serpentine tongue.

H. R. Giger's book *Species Design* contains dozens of photographs of the artist's original sketches and designs for the Sil creature (Giger 1995). Sketches of the soon-to-be chupacabra's long, thin fingers and claws appear on page 24; the goatsucker's distinctive feather-textured spine spikes can be seen on the *Species* creature on pages 25 through 29 and throughout the book; the large wraparound eyes that Tolentino reported on the chupacabra appear on pages 51, 52, and 53; the earless, oblong head appears on page 33 and elsewhere; and so on. Though there are a few minor differences, the similarity of the Sil creature from the *Species* film to the Puerto Rican chupacabra is clear, direct, and unmistakable. The specific details of the creature's body are very similar, as the following figures show (fig. 37).

The similarities are even more striking when you consider all the possible body features and morphological characteristics that distinguish the Sil/chupacabra form from those of other animals. Only a few animals in the world are bipedal; both Sil and Tolentino's chupacabra are; most animals have tails; neither Sil nor the chupacabra does. The creature's eyes could have been just

Figures 37A and 37B. Creature characteristics shared by the Sil *Species* alien and Tolentino's chupacabra. Illustration by the author.

about any shape, size, color, and location on the head; Sil and the chupacabra are identical, and unlike any other animal. The signature pattern of spikes down the chupacabra's spine is also unlike any known animal in the world, and exactly like the Sil alien.

Behavior

The parallels grow even stronger when we consider how Tolentino described the chupacabra's actions: She described it as hissing—something the Sil creature does in the film—and also Sil leaping fantastic distances with superhuman agility—something the creature also does.

Origins

The Sil and chupacabra creatures even have identical origin stories. As discussed in chapter 1, the two main explanations for the chupacabra are that it is either an extraterrestrial alien life form, or the result of top-secret U.S.

government genetics experiments gone wrong. These happen to be *exactly* the two origin explanations of the *Species* creature: Sil is *both* an extraterrestrial alien life form *and* the result of top-secret U.S. government genetics experiments gone wrong. The parallels could not be clearer.[5]

Timing

Species was released in the United States (including Puerto Rico) on July 7, 1995—just before the Puerto Rican chupacabra hysteria reached new heights, and less than month before Tolentino had her alleged chupacabra sighting.

The Realism of *Species*

The influence of the *Species* film on the popular depiction of the goatsucker is unmistakable. But how did a movie monster come to be seen as the dreaded chupacabra? Could Tolentino have made the leap from seeing an alien in a movie theater to seeing it stalk the Puerto Rican countryside?

In analyzing the influence of *Species* on Puerto Ricans' concept of the chupacabra, it is important to recognize that the film was designed to be very realistic. Great pains were taken by all involved, from the screenwriter to the director to the special effects staff, to make the film (and especially the starring creature) as realistic as possible.

Species is not set in some galaxy far, far away, nor in replicant-ridden 2019 Los Angeles. The film is set in the (then) present day of 1995, and the very first scene of the film is of a real radio telescope—in Puerto Rico, no less—the Arecibo Radio Observatory. For people living in Puerto Rico at the time, the film was essentially set in their home town, and *at the time they were seeing the film*. The connection to real Puerto Rican lives may have seemed quite real to some. It also helped that *Species*—a film with more gore than most science-fiction films—was not marketed as a horror film and thus attracted a larger and more diverse audience than a straight horror film would have (aimed largely at a young male demographic). Producer Frank Mancuso Jr. said this marketing was done deliberately: "With films like *Species*, we are finding ways to introduce horrific elements into movies without being labeled as exploitative, and consequently, getting an audience that, under normal circumstances, would probably never consider seeing a horror film" (Shapiro 1995b).

The film's special effects were state of the art, led by Academy Award winner Richard Edlund (who also did visual effects work on the *Star Wars* trilogy, *Raiders of the Lost Ark*, and many other films), and Emmy winner Steve Johnson of XFX, Inc.

I interviewed Joe Fordham, the production coordinator for *Species*, who worked with Giger and was consulted on some of Giger's earliest renderings of the Sil character. "The whole thing of the spikes and the way Sil's hair was articulated all just flowed out of the look of the character," he told me. "What you saw in those early drawings, particularly the way the back spines came out and the way they flowed in the same lines as the hair with dreadlock look to them—all that came from Giger and Steve brought that to reality, and Richard Edlund interpreted that as well" (Fordham 2009).

For the film, Edlund pioneered a then-new technique of using puppets for motion capture. The resulting Sil alien was depicted with a combination of live actors, animatronic puppets, computer-generated imagery (CGI), and models. According to Edlund, "We wanted Sil to be able to move in non-human ways, leaping around and climbing walls and doing things like that." The filmmakers used puppets to achieve the required dexterity for the alien; visual effects designer John Mann said that "[w]ith Sil, the crux of the animation issue was how to make Giger's essentially humanoid form move in non-human ways." Most people who reported seeing the chupacabra claimed its movement was just that: A humanoid form moving in nonhuman ways (hopping, leaping, flying, etc.) (*Species* press kit 1995).

The result was a creature far more realistic and lifelike than any before seen on film before 1995 (Shay 1995). According to Edlund, the special effects on *Species* were "past anything that had ever been done before. It is like building a new violin and learning to play it. With today's equipment and technology, we can do things we couldn't have even dreamed of even two years ago." As Steve Johnson noted, "In *Species*, nothing we did was standard technique—but it was, hands down, the best work we've ever done" (*Species* press kit 1995).

Even the *Species* story itself heavily borrows from reality and plausible science. There is, in fact, a government project to search for extraterrestrial alien life (the SETI program), which has used Puerto Rico's Arecibo observatory. Scientists have, in fact, sent out coded messages to whatever intelligences may be out there, giving information about humans. Screenwriter Feldman says he wrote *Species* "as a thinking person's horror film." Indeed, Feldman says he went to great pains to make sure that the film was as realistic and plausible as he could make it: "Roger [Mancuso, the producer] wanted me to substantiate all the science and the reality in the film. So I spent a lot of time talking to my scientist friends and reading books to make sure that everything in the film would be possible and accurate" (Shapiro 1995a).

By mixing actual events, real places, and real science with possible events and speculative science, Feldman achieved a very high degree of credibility. This blurring of the line between fact and fiction, between science fiction and reality, helped propel *Species* into the Puerto Rican consciousness.

For the alien to leap from the silver screen to the Puerto Rican countryside, it was not necessary for all Puerto Ricans, most, or even a few to believe that what was seen in the movie was real. It only took one influential person, one seminal description (and some good publicity) to forever crystallize the chupacabra's form in the public's mind.

Let's return to Madelyne Tolentino. There is a direct connection between the film *Species* and the Puerto Rican version of the chupacabra, but just because the film was being screened in Puerto Rico right before the chupacabra was first sighted doesn't absolutely prove that Tolentino's eyewitness description of her chupacabra sighting was influenced by the film. Unless we know for certain that Tolentino saw the movie—and was thus exposed to its very chupacabra-like alien—prior to her seeing the creature, the link is strong but not conclusive.

As it happens, Madelyne Tolentino stated that she saw the film *Species* before her chupacabra sighting. The smoking gun appears in a March 1996 interview with Lucy Plá and José Manuel Rodriguez. It is reprinted as chapter 5 in Scott Corrales's book *Chupacabras and Other Mysteries*.

Tolentino states that she saw "a movie called *Species*. It would be a very good idea if you saw it. The movie begins here in Puerto Rico, at the Arecibo observatory. There's an experiment going on in the film, a girl in a glass box as a result of the experiment . . . When they try to kill her with poison gases, she breaks the box with supernatural strength. What came out from inside the girl made my hair stand on end. It was a creature that looked like the chupacabra, with spines on its back and all. . . . The resemblance to the chupacabra was really impressive" (Corrales 1997).

The logical implication, that the film's monster's being identical to the chupacabra Tolentino later claimed to see is a cause-and-effect relationship instead of an amazing coincidence, seems to have escaped chupacabra researchers. Later in the interview Tolentino states, "I watched the movie and wondered, 'My God! How can they make a movie like that, when these things are happening in Puerto Rico?'"

What are we to make of this statement?

At first it may seem like Tolentino was saying nothing more significant than that certain aspects of what she had seen in the film reminded her of what was happening in real life in Puerto Rico at that time. (For example, it would be like an American audience in 2008 watching the film *The Hurt Locker*, about a bomb disposal expert in the Iraq War: though the movie is clearly fictional, it is set in a real place and has elements of real life.)

But a closer reading of the interview suggests instead that Tolentino *believed that what she saw in the film was actually happening in real life*. She is then asked a follow-up question about the film: "In other words, does [*Species*] make you think there might have been an experiment in which a being escaped and is now at large [in Puerto Rico]?"

Tolentino responded, "Yes, but they managed to kill her in the movie. . . . Look, a journalist told me that El Yunque [jungle wildlife refuge in Puerto Rico, said to be the chupacabra's origin] was allegedly closed down because of the damage caused by Hurricane Hugo. He told me that the truth was that some experiment had escaped—not monkeys or anything like that. They never found those creatures. The journalist . . . knows a lot about it, because he's been researching this for a while." Note that the interview was conducted in Puerto Rico in 1996, less than a year after Tolentino's sighting—therefore when the questioner, Lucy Plá, refers to events in the present tense ("and is now at large") she is referring to a time when chupacabra reports were flourishing in Puerto Rico.[6]

I believe it is clear that Tolentino believed that the creatures and events she saw in a science-fiction thriller movie were actually happening in reality at the time in Puerto Rico. Tolentino regarded *Species*, if not as a documentary, at least as a fictionalized account of obviously real events. This confusion between fact and fiction, reality and fantasy, says much about her credibility.[7]

The most influential chupacabra eyewitness in history described something she'd seen in a movie as the mysterious beast she encountered in real life. The fact that it took fifteen years to discover this stunning piece of information is curious as well. Perhaps the chupacabra researchers, recognizing that their gold-standard eyewitness account had serious credibility problems, chose not to look too closely at her story. Or perhaps no one bothered to do any real research or investigation. After all, it's much easier to simply collect stories and reprint news reports than to actually verify the accuracy of those accounts.

Whatever the reason, this revelation leaves a gaping hole at the heart of chupacabra research. With the original and "standard" chupacabra eyewitness and description discredited, later sightings that agreed with her description are clearly suspect. Either those witnesses also saw *Species* and adapted their descriptions to fit the film, as Tolentino did, or their perceptions were heavily influenced by Tolentino's widely publicized description. Either way, the reports cannot be considered evidence independently confirming an objective description of a creature from Tolentino's imagination or memories of a film she saw, any more than someone could "confirm" Tolentino's mistaken memory of meeting a celebrity or living aboard the Starship *Enterprise*.

The Psychology of Confabulation

To some with a scant knowledge of psychology, the idea that a person could or would confuse something they saw in a movie with something they personally experienced in real life is less believable than the existence of an unknown goatsucking vampire. However, a robust body of studies shows that exactly such a phenomenon can and does happen—and probably more often than people realize. It could be as simple as "remembering" a personal, firsthand experience from your childhood that you were merely told about (but were not present for).

The process of confusing events that we have seen on television or in films (or even have been told about) for actual, firsthand experiences, is called confabulation. Assuming that Tolentino genuinely believes that her chupacabra encounter was real (and I believe she does), her experience is a classic example of false memory. Researchers such as Elizabeth Loftus have demonstrated that memories of things that never happened can be implanted (or accidentally created) rather easily (Loftus 1980). Many people claim to have been abducted by extraterrestrials, to have experienced past lives, and so on (see Taub 1999; Hirstein 2006; and Sabbagh 2009). In most of these cases, the person is sincere in their belief, convinced that their memories could not be in error or created by imagination.

For example, researchers at the University of Warwick conducted experiments to see if they could create false eyewitness testimony using faked videotapes (Wade, Green, and Nash 2009). In a study published in the journal *Applied Cognitive Psychology*, subjects viewed a digitally faked videotape of something they had personally experienced, and were asked to confirm whether or not the tape was accurate. Those who visually experienced the actions on the tape were three times more likely to affirm the accuracy of the faked tape than controls who were merely told what the tape showed. This experiment demonstrates that some subjects incorporated what they saw on a television screen into their "real" memories and, when given a choice between relying on what they actually remembered and what they saw represented as reality, they chose the latter. Researchers concluded that "showing potential witnesses fabricated evidence—or perhaps even genuine evidence that is somehow misleading—might induce them to testify about entire experiences they have never actually had." This result is of course not exactly the same as believing that an obviously fictional film represents reality, but the psychological processes are similar. There are several examples in the world of cryptozoology (or monster research) in which eyewitnesses have reported encountering creatures, aliens, and monsters that they actually saw only in films.

Steve Feltham, who has lived on the shores of Loch Ness since 1991 and is the world's only full-time Nessie researcher, states that many "eyewitness" sightings of Scotland's famous lake monster can be traced back directly to Hollywood movies. He has no doubt that eyewitnesses sometimes describe seeing things that they only really saw in fiction. When I interviewed him in 2006, he asked me, "You remember the movie here on the loch that came out ten years ago? The one with Ted Danson? Well, there's a scene at Urquhart Castle that shows two Nessies there with long, thin necks." That scene, Feltham told me, changed descriptions of what people saw on the loch. All of a sudden eyewitnesses started reporting seeing monsters with necks exactly as depicted in the film. They had seen the film and either consciously or subconsciously decided that that was what the monster looked like. When they later saw something they couldn't identify out on the lake, their minds filled in details from the movies. "Nobody reported seeing twenty-foot-long necks until after that film came out," he said (Feltham 2006). Unless the Nessie monsters had somehow seen the film and changed their appearance to fit what people were expecting them to look like, this is a clear example of how pop culture influences people's expectations and even their sightings.

In 2009 Canadian researcher and *Skeptic* magazine editor Daniel Loxton investigated reports of a monster in British Columbia's Thetis Lake. It was 1972, and according to several books, the monster was described by eyewitnesses as a fishlike humanoid "with silvery scaled skin, sharp claws, and spikes on its head." Two teenagers saw the creature emerge from the lake and look around; a newspaper headline the next day read, "Thetis Monster Seen by Boys." According to one eyewitness, Mike Gold, the creature "was shaped like an ordinary body, like a human being body but it had a monster face and it was all scaly." Furthermore, the scary beast had "a point sticking out of its head" and "great big ears." Several authors of monster-themed tomes cited the case in their books as a genuine mystery, possibly representing a new type of lake creature.

Other than the pair of seemingly sincere eyewitnesses, there was no evidence of the creature. Nothing of that size or shape had ever been seen in the man-made lake before or since, and the incident was bizarre. Loxton noted that the Thetis Lake monster's visage seemed outlandish and suspiciously cinematic (almost like *The Creature from the Black Lagoon*), and wondered if somehow the boys' description of the monster had been influenced by something they had seen or heard.

After careful research, Loxton found something very interesting: Though *The Creature from the Black Lagoon* had not been shown recently in Victoria, British Columbia, a very similar low-budget knockoff, *Monster from the Surf*, had. In fact, as Loxton discovered, "*Monster from the Surf* played twice one weekend—and the first Thetis Lake monster sighting was reported within a week! That's right: local TV showed a monster movie about a scaled, humanoid gill-man attacking teenagers at the beach after dark. Four days later, local teenagers reported being attacked at the Thetis beach after dark by a scaled monster!" (Loxton 2009).

Furthermore, the boys' description of the monster they saw exactly matched the creature in *Monster from the Surf*, down to the point on the creature's head and the large, ear-like gills. This is an open-and-shut case of people's taking their detailed eyewitness description of a supposedly real, mysterious monster directly out of a movie. When Loxton contacted one of the now-grown men about their sighting decades later—something no other researcher had done before—the man admitted it was all a hoax. They had in fact described the monster they had seen in the film, and pretended they saw it in real life.

So again we return to Tolentino. Did she make the story up? Did she dream the whole experience, and convince herself and others that it was real? Did she actually see some animal or person or object she didn't recognize, and unconsciously fill in the details with memories of the monster from the *Species* film? Did she actually see a chupacabra that, by some astronomically unlikely coincidence, just happened to look exactly like a monster in a film she'd recently seen? Was it all a hoax? Short of a confession, there's no way to know for certain what happened, but it seems clear that the most important chupacabra description cannot be trusted.

The Problem of Eyewitnesses

Though Tolentino's sighting was the most influential, it was of course not the only one. What of the handful of "credible" eyewitness accounts in Puerto Rico? Less-than-skeptical researcher Scott Corrales describes the "serious, genuine, and often frightened witnesses who had seen the strange creature . . . with their own eyes. Although some of the things they described seem impossible, investigators who have interviewed them find it extremely difficult to disbelieve them because they are so obviously concerned and serious, and they stick to their stories, even in the face of ridicule" (Corrales 1997, 31).

Corrales makes a common and basic research error, not realizing that "serious, genuine, and often frightened witnesses" can simply be mistaken. Very few of the chupacabra reports are suspected hoaxes; in virtually all of the cases, the eyewitnesses seem serious and sincere because they *are* serious and sincere. Serious, genuine, and sincere people make mistakes. Good, honest people make errors and misunderstand things. The strength with which one holds a belief has no bearing on the validity of that belief.

Psychology helps us understand the processes that lead people to misperceive and misunderstand things they see. These processes are especially obvious in the case of chupacabra reports. The eyewitness reports simply cannot all be true or accurate, since they vary so widely and are often contradictory. As I noted earlier, the chupacabra cannot both have a tail and *not* have a tail; it cannot have wings and *not* have wings. No matter how sincere the eyewitnesses, some people—perhaps many or even all of them—must be wrong, either in their descriptive reports or in assuming that what they saw was the chupacabra. Corrales's faith in eyewitnesses notwithstanding, they cannot all be correct.

As we have seen, the original chupacabra report and its globally disseminated description come from a woman who got her facts wrong and confused fantasy with reality, and whose story could not be supported or corroborated by any other eyewitnesses or evidence. Most monster researchers and writers are, of course, loathe to dismiss Tolentino's eyewitness report. After all, it is the most famous and influential chupacabra sighting in history, and if it can be effectively discredited, then we must also question the validity of every similar chupacabra report in its wake. With much of the evidence relying so heavily on eyewitness testimony, the Puerto Rican chupacabra collapses like a house of cards. Writers like Loren Coleman, Scott Corrales, Jeff Meldrum, Michael Newton, and many others have argued for decades that eyewitness testimony is valid and reliable, scoffing at skeptics such as myself who continually point to a massive body of evidence showing that sincere, credible eyewitnesses are often simply wrong. The chupacabra presents an embarrassing conundrum, for those who believe in it must either admit that dozens of sincere, credible eyewitnesses who repeated or expanded on Tolentino's fictional account merely imagined the chupacabra based on cues from her widely circulated sketch, or that it is a complete coincidence that Tolentino's description of the chupacabra is virtually identical to the creature she and others saw in a film at the same time. There's really no way to put a good face on it: this case proves beyond any doubt how wrong first-person eyewitness reports can be.

Because of the lack of hard evidence for creatures such as Bigfoot and chupacabra, Corrales (and indeed most other cryptozoological researchers) are forced to put great weight on anecdotes and eyewitness accounts. If they were to acknowledge how fundamentally error-prone eyewitness accounts are (a fact well known to many, including psychologists and police detectives), they would be in effect discrediting the vast majority of their evidence.

It is curious that many aspects of Tolentino's sighting were not investigated by researchers at the time. For example, though Tolentino's 1996 interview claims that her mother and a young neighbor boy both saw the creature, neither was interviewed. There is also no hard physical evidence of the chupacabra's visit. Furthermore, several parts of Tolentino's account are contradictory, outlandish, or simply incredible. The complete lack of any credible investigation into this important claim does not bode well for other Puerto Rican chupacabra claims around the same time. How meticulous and thorough could the other chupacabra sighting investigations have been, if researchers (mostly UFO buffs) failed to do even follow-up interviews and rudimentary investigation on the most important case?

Other Eyewitnesses

Those who are convinced that some real mysterious creature was being seen in Puerto Rico must address two fatal flaws in their theory. Researchers such as Scott Corrales dismiss skeptical explanations, asking, "If the Puerto Rican chupacabra was some sort of collective delusion or mass hysteria, then what were people seeing in all those reports?" This seems like a valid and legitimate question—until you realize that chupacabra *sightings* are not the same thing as chupacabra *reports*. As noted earlier, actual *sightings* of a strange creature (of whatever description) are relatively rare, and were rare even in 1995 and 1996 Puerto Rico. Far more often the chupacabra's presence was inferred or assumed following the discovery of "mysteriously" killed animals. So the question "What were all the eyewitnesses seeing in all those reports?" is based upon a faulty premise: Most people who reported the chupacabra never claimed to actually see it at all.

Furthermore, Corrales exaggerates the number and the consistency of chupacabra reports in 1995–1996 Puerto Rico. In a May 2010 Cryptomundo. com posting he wrote, "To pin the entire narrative of the chupacabras on a single set of witnesses (Ms. Tolentino and her husband) is to deny the hundreds of eyewitness accounts from all over Puerto Rico at the time that described the same creature." Corrales offers no proof or evidence of these "hundreds of eyewitness accounts from all over Puerto Rico" that described the same creature that Tolentino saw. They do not appear in his most comprehensive book on the subject, *Chupacabras and Other Mysteries*, nor did Corrales reply to my public request for any references or sources for his information. (Loren Coleman, for his part, also seems unaware of the "hundreds" of cases that Corrales refers to, mentioning instead "a relatively small number of sightings of an upright gray, spiky haired primate in Puerto Rico" [2009].)

Corrales seems to hope that readers will simply accept his statements and statistics as true because he said so—a leap of faith that I for one am unwilling to make, given the vast amounts of error and misinformation surrounding the chupacabra. Until and unless he makes available some or all of the "hundreds" of eyewitness sighting reports he believes exist, we are left with only a handful of *Species*-like chupacabra sightings, which can in fact be attributed to psychological processes such as modeling, mass hysteria, and the power of suggestion.

There is an even more powerful and basic argument that a population of unknown, rarely detected creatures that Tolentino described did not exist in Puerto Rico at the time: they would have been sighted routinely. To understand why, you simply have to look at Puerto Rican geography and demographics. While some may imagine Puerto Rico as a large, sparsely populated Caribbean jewel, the island is very small, about 3,500 square miles. Puerto Rico is only about the size of Connecticut, yet it is home to nearly four million people. It has a population density of 1,113 people per square mile, making it the second most densely populated state or commonwealth in the United States.

While it is true that some of the island is rural and covered with vegetation, there would literally be no place for a group of five-foot-tall mystery beasts to hide on the island. Unless chupacabras have the ability to turn

Figure 38. The El Yunque rainforest in eastern Puerto Rico, said to be birthplace of the chupacabra. Photo by the author.

invisible, they would have been seen much more often, and their victims would have appeared far more frequently. So where were they? Two popular theories about where the chupacabra might have been able to live undetected (except for rare appearances) include in the El Yunque rainforest on the eastern end of the island, and in the handful of caves that dot the island. At first glance these hiding places might seem plausible, except that El Yunque, though a sizeable park at 28,000 acres, is also the most popular tourist spot in Puerto Rico, attracting over one million visitors each year. That's an average of nearly three thousand tourists walking and hiking in El Yunque every day, and more than eighty thousand each month. Yet apparently not a single tourist reported seeing, photographing, or being attacked by a chupacabra (nor, to my knowledge, finding the alleged chupacabra victim carcasses that would presumably litter the rainforest floor). It beggars belief to think that one or more chupacabras managed to live for years in such a heavily traveled area without ever being discovered or leaving traces of their existence.

Puerto Rico's caves seem a far more likely bet, and it may be significant that the "chupacabra" in the *Species* film is cornered and confronted in a subterranean, cavelike lair. However no chupacabras have been reported in the caves, nor has any evidence of a suspected chupacabra nest or lair been found. In Mexico at the height of the chupacabra panic some farmers set fires in caves, hoping to kill or smoke out the beast from its assumed lair. Though no goatsuckers were found or harmed, there were real victims of this belief: the fire and smoke killed bats and destroyed their native habitats.

8

The Zoology of Chupacabras
and the Science of Vampires

Bit by bit each piece of the chupacabra puzzle comes together. The original 1995 Puerto Rican chupacabra sightings have been discredited. Scientific analysis of alleged chupacabra carcasses have turned out to be those of normal animals. If careful examination of the evidence shows that the chupacabra probably does not exist except as a sociocultural entity and a figment of cinematic imagination, then what killed the chupacabra victims? It seems *something* was killing (and sucking blood from) various animals—if not the chupacabra, then what? And why? The vampirism claims remain the sole unexplained mystery.

What can we make of the dozens of claims made by farmers and ranchers that they found livestock drained of every drop of blood? Here is a sample from Scott Corrales, italics mine throughout: "Fifty goats had been slain in the town of Comerio, and the creature responsible had been identified as three feet tall and hairy. The means by which the animals had been slain was common to all others on the island—incisions around the neck, *through which blood had been extracted*, and, in some cases, the absence of certain organs, such as the heart and the liver" (Corrales 1997, 16). The experience of cattleman Don Francisco Ruiz, a resident of Humacao on the eastern shore, is typical. He "was stunned to discover, on the morning of May 22 [1995], that three of his goats and their young lay dead *without a drop of blood in their bodies* . . . Puncture marks were discovered in the goats' necks, foreheads, and legs. The result of Mr. Ruiz's crude autopsies on his animals, performed on the spot, demonstrated beyond any doubt that the *carcasses had been completely emptied of blood*" (17).

Throughout Corrales's book, cursory claims of complete desanguination appear over and over: "there was *not a single drop of blood to be seen . . ."* (63); "The wounds inflicted on the hapless goat 'were precise and without any rending' . . . and *had inexplicably lost all their blood"* (71); "fifteen guinea hens *completely bloodless"* (75); "a 150-pound sheep was found dead and *drained of all its blood"* (76); "five chickens *entirely drained of blood"* (78); and so on. In case after case, the "bloodless" claim appears.

The majority of the claims of bloodless corpses came from the tabloid *El Vocero*. Over and over, Puerto Ricans were told what to expect in a suspected chupacabra attack aftermath—and the most common feature was also the one most difficult to verify or prove: blood loss. It's fairly easy to determine if an animal is dead; a kick or foot nudge will tell you, if the stench of decay doesn't tip you off. But determining how much blood the animal has in its body is far more difficult.

Little wonder, then, that as the chupacabra hysteria snowballed, the tabloid reports, rumor, and gossip created an expectant attention. Puerto Ricans who found dead animals that had fallen to some predator simply began *assuming* that the animal(s) had been drained of blood. There was little interest or need to actually go to the considerable trouble and expense of medically verifying the fact. Besides, it is likely that if the animals' owner expressed any doubts that their animals had been vampirized, the tabloid reporter would have no reservations about massaging the facts and selecting the quotes that would make for a better story. A farmer or housewife who excitedly swears that the goat they found had absolutely been drained of every single drop of blood makes for a better story than one who isn't sure (or who admits he or she didn't really look).

In his book *Chupacabras And Other Mysteries*, Scott Corrales quotes a news story from *El Vocero* in which Angela Lajes, a housewife in Ponce, claimed that her sister, Angela Santiago, "told her that two cats on her property had been found entirely dry, as if they had nothing inside them" (Corrales 1997, 72). Note that the information Corrales is presenting as a presumably factual chupacabra report is fourth-hand: Corrales is reporting *what a journalist says* that Angela Lajes *told him about what her sister told her* about the condition of two cats! The credibility of this sort of account is so poor it would hardly even qualify as a bad urban legend. It is amazing that Corrales, or anyone else, would accept this type of account at face value, yet it is presented as another example of the chupacabra mystery.

Second, and perhaps more tellingly, the reader is left to wonder how, exactly, Angela Santiago determined that the two cats she found were "entirely dry." Did this housewife gut her cats with a kitchen knife to perform a crude autopsy? Did she squeeze the dead cats to see if any blood came out? Did she simply look at the cats and for some unknown reason conclude that every drop of blood had been drained from them? Or did the *El Vocero* tabloid reporter introduce that detail himself to make the event all the more mysterious and sensational? This type of report is typical of unsupported claims about desiccated animals.

Indeed, many chupacabra reports do not even involve the goatsucker's victims having been claimed to be drained of blood. For example, one man outside of El Paso in January 2010 said he believed a chupacabra had killed his chickens—not because they had been drained of blood, which reporters and photographs proved they clearly were not—but merely because he had expected to find more blood at the scene (Koester 2010). Chupacabra reports and claims have become so generalized and amorphous that they no longer even necessarily involve blood loss.

Those who find the dead animals are never forensic or medical experts; instead they are often farmers and ranch hands. The question of what killed an animal is, after all, ultimately a medical and forensic issue. Those who find the chupacabra victims claim a variety of unusual things, such as that the animals are drained of blood, or have two bite marks on their necks. Wild dog and coyotes may attack livestock, they say, but they don't suck the blood out of their victims!

The key to solving this mystery lies in examining the vampirism claim, because that is the defining characteristic of the dead animals, and of the chupacabra. If the blood-draining claims are true, then there is a real mystery. But if they are not—if the claims are simply mistakes or misunderstandings— then the mystery vanishes and we are left with ordinary animal attacks.

How could the animals be drained of blood? The answer is, they weren't. No medical expert has independently confirmed claims that the chupacabra victims were in fact sucked dry by some bloodthirsty beast. So what's going on?

What about the chupacabras found in Texas and elsewhere? None of the carcasses had any physiological features that would allow them to suck blood. In fact, a simple look at the canid mouth demonstrates that it is physically impossible for adult coyotes and dogs to suck blood. It cannot be done; it is a question of basic physics and simple anatomy. Suction requires an imbalance of pressure. A liquid or gas is drawn from one space to another; when you suck on a straw in a soft drink, you suck in your cheeks to create negative pressure, and the drink is drawn upward through the straw. This works because humans have cheeks, small forward-facing mouths, and pliable lips that can create a seal and therefore suction. The mouth and jaw structures of adult dogs, coyotes, and other canids prevent them from creating a seal, and therefore physically prevent them from "sucking" anything. Count Dracula could pull it off, using his teeth to pierce the veins and his mouth to draw the blood, but chupacabras could not.

Thus it would be impossible for any of the recovered suspected chupacabra animals to have sucked the blood out of goats or anything else. Phylis Canion's chupacabras would not be able to suck blood, nor could Jorge Talavera's animal, nor the Blanco beast, nor any of the others. No matter what other mysteries they may try to find or create surrounding their animals, the basics of anatomy and physics prove that none of the animals could be the goatsucking chupacabra.

The Mouths of True Vampires

Unlike the European villagers who exhumed poor Peter Plogojowitz in 1725 to find out if he might be a vampire, we can use modern science to answer that question. Vampires—animals that suck blood—are referred to in zoology as hematophagous. Most of the world's bloodsucking animals are insects, such as bedbugs, (female) mosquitoes, sandflies, fleas, lice, ticks, and assassin bugs. Vampirism can also be found in marine animals (such as leeches and lampreys, for example), though the most familiar bloodsucker is probably the vampire bat. Regardless of the type of animal, hematophagous organisms have developed distinctive, specialized mouth structures to drain blood from their prey. Host animals are of course unlikely to volunteer their precious lifeblood, and therefore vampiric animals have evolved ways to penetrate the skin and flesh of their hosts. Leeches and lampreys, for example, have strong suckers that allow them to attach to other animals. Mosquitoes have tiny, sharp probisces (hollow, needle-like mouth structures) that create a puncture wound from which to draw blood. The chupacabra is, however, obviously not an insect.

The vampiric animal most like the canid is the vampire bat (*Desmodus rotundus*), which technically does not "suck" blood but instead bites its victim with sharp teeth and laps at the blood as it oozes out of the wound. Special enzymes in the bat's saliva act as anticoagulants (to keep the blood flowing freely) and anesthetic to keep the wound painless. Bat teeth also lack enamel, and self-sharpen every time the bat takes a bite.

Figure 39. Vampire bat preying on the neck of a deer. Photograph by the author.

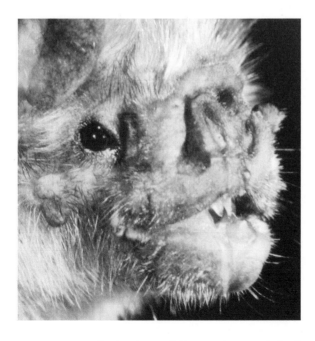

Figure 40. The mouth of the vampire bat has specialized features that allow it to suck blood. Author photo of display at the Bat Jungle History Museum, Monteverde, Costa Rica.

The "chupacabras" found in Texas and elsewhere are from the Canidae family, and therefore have canine teeth (fangs). But blood cannot be sucked through those fangs. We turn once again to biology and zoology to see what sorts of animals suck blood through fangs. The answer is none; there are no animals that drain blood through their teeth. Ben Speers-Roesch, who holds a PhD in Comparative Biochemistry and Physiology from the University of British Columbia, has never heard of any blood-drinking animals with hollow teeth. "I don't think there are any," he told me. "All of them [hematophagous mammals] simply cause a wound that bleeds (helped by secreted anticoagulants) and then lap/suck it up. I don't think it would be very effective to suck blood through hollow teeth and, anyway, where would it go after that? A toothed vertebrate would have to evolve new connections in the jawbone to the digestive tract" (Speers-Roesch 2010). None of the alleged chupacabra carcasses has hollow teeth or specialized jaw structures that would draw the blood into the stomach. Some animals do have hollow (or grooved) teeth or tooth-like appendages, for example venomous snakes and spiders. But those specialized dental adaptations are used to *inject* fluids (i.e., poison), not suck them out.

Drinking blood is one thing, but digesting it as a food source is a very different matter. Because blood is so rich in iron—and because the body has difficulty excreting excess iron—any animal that consumes blood regularly runs a very real risk of iron overdose. While iron is necessary for all animals (and indeed most life), in high doses it can be toxic. This condition, called haemochromatosis, can cause a wide variety of diseases and problems, including liver damage, buildup of fluid in the lungs, dehydration, low blood pressure, and nervous disorders.

The bodies of vampiric animals also have adapted specialized digestive mechanisms. Leeches, for example, store consumed blood in their bodies for later digestion. This requires the leeches' body to secrete specialized enzymes, as well as antibiotics, to keep the blood fresh and free of disease-carrying bacteria. As for the vampire bat, "it requires an enormous intake of iron, which helps make hemoglobin for carrying oxygen from the lungs to the body tissues. Yet the iron intake is generally higher than what the bat needs, so it has a special process for secreting the excess. When ingested, the blood goes through a tract that's adapted for extracting nutrients. Research on this system suggests that bats have a mucous membrane along the intestinal tract that acts as a barrier to prevent too much iron from getting into their bloodstreams. They also appear to have numerous capillaries at work absorbing the blood more quickly into the system . . . The hematophagous vampire's body would have to adapt in order to survive, using only the particular proteins, enzymes, and nutrients carried in blood in its digestion" (Ramsland 2002, 35).

We can therefore derive a set of physiological characteristics of animals *known* to be vampires and compare it to found animals *suspected* of being vampires—specifically the various canid chupacabras found in the United States. If these creatures truly are the bloodsucking chupacabras they are claimed to be, their digestive systems would have had to adapt to a diet of blood. They should have identical (or very similar) enzymes and antibiotics, as well as distinctive mucous membranes lining their intestines that prevent iron toxicity. Their saliva should also differ from ordinary canid saliva, and contain the anticoagulant and anesthetic properties that would help allow it to suck blood. Furthermore, the chupacabra's mouth would have to have either hollow teeth that would allow blood to be drained from its prey, or a mouth structure able to create a vacuum to suck out the blood.

The fact that none of these structures has been found in the bodies of any "chupacabra" carcasses is fairly definitive scientific proof that the animals do not suck blood, and therefore cannot be chupacabras. Of course it's possible that at some point in the future someone will find a suspected chupacabra that has the anatomical and physiological signs of a vampire. Or, if someone captures a suspected chupacabra alive, it could be studied in captivity to see if it actually attacks animals and drinks their blood as claimed.

The Illusion of Vampirism

To understand how an animal that has been killed by a normal predator such as a dog or coyote can appear to the average person to be drained of blood, we must understand a bit about forensic investigation. When a rancher or farmer finds an animal that he or she suspects may be killed by a chupacabra, do they immediately call the police or a veterinarian to examine the animal? No. Do they butcher the animal on the spot to check if there is any blood left? No.

So how do people come to the conclusion that an animal has been drained of blood? There are two ways: Most of the time they simply guess. They don't see much blood around the outside of the animal, and assume that the animal's blood must have been sucked out by its attacker. The identification that a chupacabra was present is almost always merely a hunch, guess, or suspicion.

Occasionally, however, if the rancher is feeling especially curious (or morbid), he may actually take a pocketknife and stab or cut the animal open to see if any blood comes out. If he does this, he will likely be in for a surprise: little or no blood will be found!

This lack of blood can seem very mysterious to most people—and certainly to a person who believes he may have had a brush with the dreaded chupacabra. But there is an interesting scientific explanation. If an animal is stabbed or cut, it bleeds. Blood spurts out because its heart is pumping, creating blood pressure that is released when veins, capillaries, or arteries are cut or ruptured. When an animal dies (whether from natural causes, from ordinary predation, or from a chupacabra) the blood stops circulating, the blood pressure drops to zero, and gravity takes over as the blood seeps and pools in the lowest parts of the body.

To find out more about this process, I contacted Dr. Clare Cunliffe, a medical investigator with the Office of Medical Investigation at the University of New Mexico. Dr. Cunliffe, a thin woman with an easy smile and clipped British accent, explained how a dead animal can seem to have been drained of blood to the untrained eye (Cunliffe 2009).

One of the best-known characteristics of what happens to bodies after death is rigor mortis, the stiffening of the muscles and joints. But along with rigor mortis there is a lesser-known process called livor mortis, and it holds the key to understanding the illusion of vampirism. As Dr. Cunliffe told me, "Livor mortis is a process that happens after death. What will happen is the blood will settle in the body in the dependent [lower] areas by gravity, and this usually starts to occur within half an hour after death. Places where the body has been lying, you'll see the blood settling. The skin will have a dusty reddish-purple coloration . . . In some cases where the animal is dying slowly, it can start to occur right around the time of death . . . As the circulation stops, blood starts to pool down in these dependent areas. After a while it becomes fixed; how quickly depends on the environmental conditions. The blood is coagulating in the vessels and also leaking out from the vessels and sinking in the soft tissue."

Beginning a few hours after an animal's death, ranchers will find very little blood in most of the body—unless they turn the animal over, exposing the underside of the body, where the blood has pooled. Of course, most people wouldn't think to flip over a dead animal (especially a large, unwieldy one such as a cow or large goat) to look for the missing blood, but that's where it is. Thus many chupacabra reports are created simply because someone is looking for blood in the wrong place (or never really looked in the first place).

In fact, even turning the animal over and cutting it open will not necessarily reveal the hidden blood. As Dr. Cunliffe explains, "In addition, because of the pressure from lying on certain surfaces [such as stones or hard ground] you may see areas where there isn't any livor mortis just because the blood vessels are compressed and the blood can't settle in those areas."

Depending on the level of livor mortis, "the livor may not be fixed; the blood has pooled in the vessels but it can still move, so you can move the body and then the blood will move and start to fix in other areas. For example if you had a body on its back the blood is pooling downwards, but then if you turn the body over and leave them lying on the front, the blood will then start to pool in the anterior parts of the body."

In a few very rare instances a person finding a presumed chupacabra victim will do more than a cursory external examination. Phylis Canion, for example, said she cut one of her chickens with a knife, and was amazed that there was little or no blood.

As Dr. Cunliffe explains, "If you are just cutting the flesh, the blood may not necessarily come out, depending on how long it has been dead, because it may be fixed in the tissues and clotted. So you may not necessarily get blood coming out just from cutting into a limb. You may just see that the muscle has its usual red color." In their book *Bodies We've Buried*, forensic pathologists Jarrett Hallcox and Amy Welch (of the National Forensic Academy, the world's top crime scene investigation training school) describe the difficulty of finding blood in bodies in which livor mortis has set in: "[One way] of collecting fluid, in this case blood, is to plunge a syringe—and we might add, a syringe the size of a gutter spike—deep into the femoral artery, at the groin area of the leg, collecting any residual blood that might still remain. Depending on how long the patient has been deceased, this 'plunging' might be done multiple times to get enough blood to send to the lab" (Hallcox and Welch 2007).

Often the claim that a chupacabra victim is "bloodless" is self-evidently false, and can be seen from merely looking at photographs of the animal being described as having been "drained of every drop of blood." In one episode of the television show *Animal X*, for example, the narrator describes "mysterious" puncture marks being shown in a necropsy video of a goat's neck that had supposedly been drained of blood. The problem is that the flesh of the poor chupacabra victim being shown is clearly filled with bright red blood! Perhaps the show's producers were hoping that no one would notice that their dramatic claims were contradicted by the video they were showing.

Concluding that an animal lacks blood is a far more difficult task than concluding that blood is present. A photograph of a bloody wound is enough to demonstrate that an animal still has blood in it, but a photograph of a clean wound (such as a puncture mark from canine teeth) does not prove there is no blood (perhaps long since clotted and coagulated) in the body.

There are other forensic factors that create the illusion of a vampiric attack as well. For example, blood will naturally begin to clot and coagulate after the animal dies, creating the appearance of a loss of blood. The blood of course hasn't gone anywhere, it has just partly dried up, and the water content has evaporated. Every time a medical pathologist, doctor, or veterinarian has examined a body of a chupacabra victim, they find nothing unusual. It's only when people with no medical knowledge do a cursory examination that the mystery is created. Scott Corrales offers the following typical brief account about alleged chupacabra victims: "The twenty lifeless animals all had the same fang-marks on their throats and had been drained of blood. By the time elements of the Civil Defense had reported to Quebradas, the dead goats were too far along the decomposition process to subject their carcasses to scientific analysis" (Corrales 2010). Corrales does not seem to notice the glaring contradiction contained in his statement: If the goat carcasses were too decomposed to be subjected to scientific analysis, there's no way that anyone could establish that the animals had in fact "been drained of blood," since they were not necropsied.

Determining Blood Loss

Clearly, simply looking at a dead chicken or goat (or poking it with a stick, nudging it with a foot, or even poking its flesh with a pocketknife) is not nearly enough investigation to tell if an animal has been drained of blood. So what would be required? A complete, professional necropsy conducted by an experienced veterinarian or medical pathologist. "In humans, if we are assessing blood loss—let's say someone has been in a traffic accident—and they may have bled at the scene, and we may not know how much blood they have lost," Dr. Cunliffe told me, "one of the ways in which you can estimate if they had significant blood loss is to look at the color of the organs. If they are very pale—for example, if the kidneys are very pale—that suggests significant blood loss, so we'd look to see is the liver pale, are the kidney and spleen pale pink or red instead of purple, which it should be, that can tell you that there has been significant blood loss somewhere else. You would have to look at the organs, take out the internal organs."

For someone to conclusively show that an animal's corpse had been drained of blood, Dr. Cunliffe said, "You'd have to know what the appearances of the organs are normally . . . the normal coloration of an organ that has not suffered blood loss, to be able to compare it to something which has, the pallor of the organs. Externally the problem is—particularly if the body is intact, and there's no blood around the area, it can be really difficult, because you get fixed livor mortis after a while, and you may not be able to see just from cutting into something a lot of blood just coming out, the blood may be clotted in the body. So it may be very difficult . . . You can look at some mucus membranes, you can look at the eyes and the mouth and look for pallor, but it would be difficult without knowing what normal is for that animal."

"So you can't just tell by looking at an animal or handling it?" I asked her.

"No, no. It's hard to tell," she replied.

"So you actually have to be an expert to determine these things?"

"Right, if you're looking at blood loss, you have to examine it."

Dr. Cunliffe notes that even in humans, "it's difficult to estimate blood loss just looking at the surface of the body because people have different skin pigmentation, so in dark-colored individuals, or a dark-colored animal, it may be very hard to see the livor mortis anyway." If it's very difficult for a trained forensic medical examiner to diagnose blood loss in a human body without performing an autopsy, it would be impossible for a person with no medical training to determine that blood had been sucked out of an animal whose skin is covered by fur or feathers. It simply cannot be done, and therefore the often-heard chupacabra claim that some animal was "drained of every drop of blood" is almost certainly false unless confirmed with a professional autopsy.

Some claim that not only the blood but entire organs are missing; if true, this is not necessarily mysterious either. Jon Downes, a researcher at the Centre for Fortean Zoology, addressed this claim in a 2008 talk (2008a). Speaking about his conclusions after returning from his first trip to Puerto Rico years earlier, he said, "I came away from the trip believing the chupacabra was a very real—though paranormal—phenomenon . . . My biggest piece of evidence for a paranormal vampire was that I had done an autopsy in a small farm in Puerto Rico . . . I cut up a dead and desiccated chicken; its liver had been removed, and there was only one exit wound." As dozens of ranchers and farmers had done before him, Downes was baffled by what he saw in the course of his crude postmortem. What on earth could have achieved such a bizarre feat?

Downes got his answer in 2003, while on an adventure at the Valley of Fire National Park in Nevada. He came across an ant's nest and noticed "a column of worker ants travelling earnestly to and from the nest. Following them I found, only a few feet away, a dead bird, or what remained of it. It was desiccated from the sun . . . To my amazement I saw that whilst the ants were obviously feeding off the unfortunate creature's carcass and carrying bits of it back to the nest, they were not leaving any marks of micropredation upon the skin or feathers. Instead, they were eating the animal from the inside out, gaining entrance and egress through the cloaca" (Downes 2008b, 42). To be fair, this explanation had been offered by skeptical writers decades earlier in the context of animal mutilations, but it wasn't until Downes saw this process for himself that he was convinced.

To his credit, he realized that he had made a mistake, a logical fallacy so common it has a name: arguing from ignorance. Downes had decided that if he couldn't think of an explanation for the de-livered chicken he had eviscerated in Puerto Rico, well, then there could be no rational explanation: it must be paranormal.

To scientifically establish what happened to a "mysteriously drained" animal, a rancher would have to call a veterinarian or medical expert to examine the body as soon as possible after its discovery. This is almost never done because of the effort involved in either loading up a dead animal and transporting it to an expert, or calling an expert out to a ranch or some remote location to examine the animal. Beyond that, unless the rancher is unusually curious or committed to really investigating the mystery, he or she is unlikely to want to pay several hundred dollars just to examine a dead animal. If the rancher has already suffered the financial loss of a market-ready animal, he is more likely to want to cut his losses than spend a few hundred more dollars to medically confirm what seems obvious: the animal was drained of blood. It's much cheaper and easier to just assume the animal was drained of blood, further assume it was a chupacabra victim, bury the carcass, and be done with it. Unfortunately, any evidence is buried along with the animals.

"Mysterious Predation"?

If the animals did not die from blood loss, what killed them? For the many owners of suspected chupacabra victims who doubt that ordinary predators killed their animals, one common question is: Why did the predator leave two puncture marks on the doomed animal's neck and not eat it? This is one of the easiest questions to answer.

Amid all the opinions, conjecture, and speculation about what dogs, coyotes, or other "normal" predators would or would not do to their prey, few people bothered to actually consult experts on the topic. Reporters and writers assumed that ranchers would somehow be able to tell the difference between natural (dog or coyote) predation and supernatural (chupacabra) predation. Yet owning or running a ranch does not necessarily make one an expert on livestock predation, any more than owning a vegetable farm makes one an expert on vegetarians. The assumption made by Phylis Canion (and many others who discover or suspect a chupacabra presence) that dogs or coyotes would not attack a goat, chicken, or other livestock animal unless it planned to eat it (or carry it off) is simply not correct.

As I researched livestock predation I realized that, with the notable exception of the suspected blood draining, the external injuries to alleged chupacabra victims are exactly the same as for those of any other animal.

Dale A. Wade is an extension wildlife specialist with the Texas Agricultural Extension Service in San Angelo, Texas, and author of *Procedures for Evaluating Predation on Livestock and Wildlife*. In his book (and in material adapted for the Texas Natural Resources Server [texnat.tamu.edu] with James E. Bowns), he discusses dog and coyote predation at length: "Coyotes are the most common and the most serious predator of livestock in the western United States. Westwide, they cause a majority of the predation losses of sheep, goats and cattle" (Wade and Bowns 1984).

Furthermore, the past two decades have seen a dramatic increase in the number of North American coyote reports. In a 2010 column for *Outside* magazine, Elizabeth Royte noted that "[i]n the past twenty years, reports of human-coyote interactions—which range from 'I saw one in my neighbor's field' to 'That rangy bastard killed Snowball'—have increased exponentially: up fourfold in Texas, for example, and 16 times in California. That's not surprising: There are more people and more coyotes out there than ever before" (Royte 2010).

Dale Wade's description of how coyotes attack their prey provides a clear explanation for the vampiric puncture wounds in the neck found on chupacabra victims: "In attacks on adult sheep and goats, coyotes typically bite the throat just behind the jaw and below the ear, although repeated bites made while shifting their hold may obscure the initial tooth punctures." Furthermore, according to Wade, coyote attacks do not necessarily result in the bloody scene one might imagine (or expect): "Death commonly results from suffocation and shock; blood loss is usually a secondary cause of death."

I confirmed this statement with Mike Bowdenchuck, state director for Texas Wildlife Services, in San Antonio, Texas. Through his faint but distinctive Texas accent, Bowdenchuck explained why chicken, goats, and other livestock are often found dead with only two puncture wounds to the neck but otherwise undisturbed. This is one of the hallmarks of a mysterious chupacabra killing—and it is also completely ordinary and explainable.

I began by telling him that in my research, I've found that (contrary to popular belief), dogs and coyotes do not always tear up the animals they kill. "Your assessment about the causes of mortality is exactly right," he told me. "Coyotes and dogs don't shred them—especially poultry, they don't shred sheep and goats, they bite them in the trachea and cause them to die and then eat what they're going to eat" (Bowdenchuck 2010).

Bowdenchuck explained that when canids (especially dogs and coyotes) attack, they often instinctually go for the throat as their prey's most vulnerable area. When the coyote bites, it pierces and crushes its victim's trachea inside the neck, rupturing arteries and blood vessels. The wounded tissue swells and becomes inflamed, thus narrowing the walls of the windpipe and cutting off oxygen. The attack may be over in a split second, and the coyote will move on to another nearby victim, and then another until it runs out of victims, gets tired, eats, or is scared away. The sheep, goats, or chickens whose throats have been crushed by the coyote's attack soon die from internal—not external— hemorrhaging, suffocation, and infection. All the deadly damage is internal, and would only be detected by a necropsy, which is almost never performed. Sometimes the dogs and coyotes eat what they just killed; sometimes they don't. Predators do not necessarily eat everything (or even anything) they kill, so it is common for canids to leave dead (but otherwise intact and undisturbed) animals at the scene.

Furthermore, the type of wound that canids inflict—puncture wounds— are by their very nature among the *least* likely to bleed. Lacerations and incisions, for example, may lead to profuse blood loss. But there's often little or no blood around wounds inflicted by dogs and coyotes, since external blood loss is not the cause of death.

To people who haven't spent years researching livestock predation, this appearance may seem very mysterious. Imagine yourself as a farmer who finds a goat or a few chickens dead. They have not been eaten, nor torn apart; there is little or no blood. The chickens might almost look as though they are sleeping. But what killed them, and why are the bodies intact? The only obvious injury is external: two vampire-like puncture wounds to the throat. Whatever attacked the chickens or goats must have sucked out all the blood! Even if you

Figure 41. Explaining the chupacabra's "mysterious" vampire attack. When a coyote or dog attacks a goat, it instinctively bites the neck of its prey. Its strong jaws crush and puncture the goat's trachea, while the canine teeth leave a pair of distinctive puncture marks on the outside of the neck. While the coyote goes on to kill other animals for food or sport, the goat begins to die from suffocation, internal hemorrhaging, and/or infection. When the goat dies, the blood pressure drops and the blood coagulates and settles in the lowest parts of the body. When a rancher finds the dead goat hours or days later, the only outward sign of death will be two puncture wounds to the neck. Illustrations by Rob Dumuhosky.

have never heard of the chupacabra, it's likely someone you know or work with has; maybe you turn to the Internet and discover that what you found matches the handiwork of the chupacabra. Indeed, many chupacabra "identifications" are based on little more than seeing the two bite marks. As one Texas man who believed that a chupacabra had attacked his chickens said, "We started looking at the bite mark and there were two. The first thing that came to our head was the chupacabras" (Reed 2010).

"I live in San Antonio," Bowdenchuck said, "and my family has seen mangy coyotes in the neighborhood that fit the description of chupacabras. The unscientific people who encounter this probably couldn't have recognized it . . . The chupacabra is just a mangy coyote . . . we have them show up in Texas regularly" (Bowdenchuck 2010).

"So if a person finds some dead animals and assumes that any ordinary predator, like a dog or coyote, would have torn it to shreds and it would have bled out, doesn't always happen?" I asked.

"Absolutely," Bowdenchuck replied. "In fact, it gets weirder. Those coyotes that have mange that bad often times their skin dries and cracks and shrivels, and their lips don't cover their teeth anymore. They walk around with their teeth showing because their skin is shriveled up. And because of that, they can't get an active grip on some animals. One aspect of the mange leads to some of the behavioral issues that you're seeing. An animal with mange is not going to eat every chicken it grabs. It's going to get into a flock of chickens and crunch one and let it go, and crunch another one, and so on. It's driven by hunger and desperation to get food from around people. That's why they show up in the places they show up . . . it's all part of a very logical progression, if you understand what makes one of these things. But by God, you can't convince the people in Texas any different!"

This explanation of the process is not idle armchair theoretical speculation, nor dismissive skeptical debunking. Bowdenchuck and others have decades of experience in rural areas across North America, and have personally documented the characteristics of coyote and dog attacks. Another researcher, writer Daniel Loxton has also seen this firsthand:

As a long-time professional shepherd, I have to say that dogs are certainly the most likely culprit [in many supposedly "mysterious" animal killings]. Wolves generally just quietly pull down a lone stray; bears just wade in, absently swat a couple (often causing severe injuries) and then walk off with one at random; dogs really will chase down many sheep just for the fun of it. This is not only common knowledge among sheep professionals, but also something I've observed first hand. We used Great Pyrenee and Hungarian Kuvasz guardian dogs in the flocks I managed. These are typically raised with the lambs, have minimal human contact, and identify strongly with—and therefore protect—the sheep. In rare cases, a young dog will exhibit too strong a chase instinct toward their lamb-brethren (not too surprising, since this is the natural drive for canines, which we have suppressed through breeding). Those dogs will start to "play" with the lambs, will be gratified by the dramatic response they get from the lambs, and a conditioning spiral takes off from there.

In one unfortunate case from my own career, a lovely fully grown pup named Twinkie decided one day to run down an almost market-ready lamb (about sixty pounds) in the pasture. This she did, killing the lamb—and suddenly beginning a daylight killing spree. I pursued the dog at high speed on a quad ATV as she got right carried away with her fun, running down one lamb after another in front of me. It was just a lark to her, but also terribly swift and efficient. In each case, she would simply bite the throat of the lamb while running, and leave it to die without even bothering to stop. I kept stopping to put down stumbling, dying lambs all the way through the back fields. She must have executed ten lambs in the space of just a few minutes, all while I was watching and screaming at her to stop. (Loxton 2007)

Thus it is not necessarily strange or mysterious that sheep, goats, or chickens would be found dead with bite marks on their necks, but otherwise untouched and uneaten. Such an animal—far from being a probable chupacabra victim—would likely have simply been attacked for sport and left to die. No vampires required.

So, to recap, coyote attacks have several characteristics: (1) they are common in the western United States; (2) they attack goats at the neck, leaving puncture wounds; and (3) the victimized animals most often die of suffocation and shock instead of blood loss. Animals killed by coyotes and dogs exhibit exactly the same puncture wounds as those "mysteriously" found on animals believed to have been killed by a chupacabra. Any connection between dead animals and the chupacabra is simply wild speculation, not a proven fact. Not a single photograph, film, or video has ever surfaced showing any suspected chupacabra sucking blood from a goat, chicken, or other animal.

In fact, an examination of photographs of alleged chupacabra victims are indistinguishable from non-chupacabra victims. I invite readers to see for themselves, using an Internet image search for photographs of animals killed by coyotes and photographs of animals said to have been killed by chupacabras. In his book (and on the website of the Texas Natural Resources Server), Wade shows photos with captions such as "The carcass of this elk calf exhibits injuries typical of predation, in this case, tooth punctures in the throat. This calf was killed and fed upon by coyotes," and "This pronghorn antelope exhibits similar injuries, punctures in the throat, typical of predation. In this case, the pronghorn was killed by a coyote." Uneaten, dead animals are killed by tooth puncture wounds to the throat.

Chupacabra proponents find the fact that dead animals are found with two (or more) puncture marks in the neck bizarre and mysterious. But this assumption simply shows their ignorance of ordinary predation: *Of course* an animal that has been attacked by another animal (mysterious or ordinary) would have teeth marks—how else would the predator attack? Humans and apes are the only animals that can attack using their hands; with a few exceptions, just about every other animal attacks with its mouth (often biting the

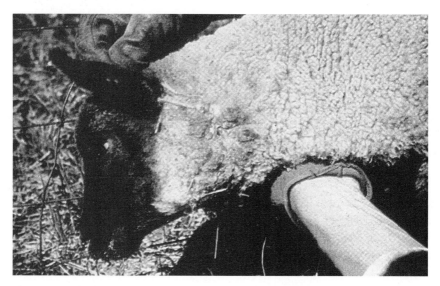

Figure 42. A lamb found dead but uneaten, the only external injury being puncture marks to the throat left by a coyote attack. From Wade and Bowns, *Procedures for Evaluating Predation on Livestock and Wildlife*, U.S. Department of the Interior.

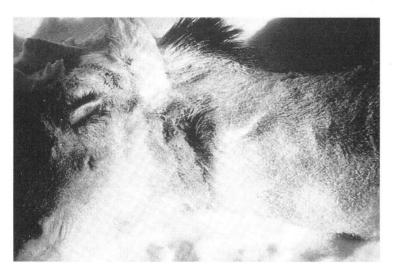

Figure 43. A pronghorn antelope killed by puncture wounds to the throat, caused by a coyote attack. From Wade and Bowns, *Procedures for Evaluating Predation on Livestock and Wildlife*, U.S. Department of the Interior.

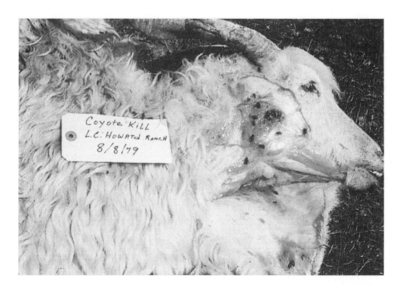

Figure 44. Injuries to this goat (tooth punctures and hemorrhage in the jaw and throat) are typical of coyote predation. Though there was little or no obvious external bleeding, removing the skin revealed significant internal bleeding. From Wade and Bowns, *Procedures for Evaluating Predation on Livestock and Wildlife*, U.S. Department of the Interior.

head or neck), which usually leaves puncture marks. There is nothing at all mysterious or vampiric about this.

Furthermore, Wade and Bowns (1984) make the point that "[a] common error made in evaluating predator kills and feeding is the tendency to stereotype these by species. Most predators do follow a general pattern, but individuals vary in food preferences, method of attack and feeding behavior." Derek Quann, resource conservation manager for Canada's Cape Breton Highland National Park, notes that anyone who says "a coyote would do this, or a coyote wouldn't do that" simply doesn't know much about coyote behavior. "The coyote is an experimenter. It will try new things, and if it succeeds it will learn that behavior and pass it on" (quoted in Royte 2010).

This is exactly the error made by Phylis Canion (and many others) when she states confidently that "[a]ny predator we have here would normally carry the game off . . . a coyote would carry the chicken off." She may be correct that *some* coyotes would do that, but that doesn't mean that most or all of them will; just because a coyote doesn't act or look according to a person's mistaken expectations doesn't make it a chupacabra. (Note that Floridian Olimpia Govea also made this same mistake; see chapter 1.)

Wade and Bowns suggest that it is virtually impossible to determine the cause of death simply by looking at a dead animal—or even handling it. Instead, to determine what killed the animal (blood loss, disease, injury, etc.), the person examining the body should "examine carcasses for wounds, hemorrhage, bruises, broken bones and feeding. If necessary, the entire carcass should be skinned and opened to identify internal wounds and other factors which help confirm the cause of death. For example, some animals are killed by a single grip at the throat which causes suffocation but leaves little external evidence. . . . Knowledge and skill are often necessary to determine the cause of injuries or death. Although direct observation of predation is rare, it is the most specific evidence possible and may also permit identification of the responsible animal. Fresh injuries or kills which exhibit tooth, claw or talon punctures and hemorrhage are also specific evidence of predation. However, it is seldom possible to identify the individual predator responsible and occasionally it is not possible to identify the species from the carcass appearance alone" (Wade and Bowns 1984).

Some who believe in the chupacabra ridicule the idea that ranchers might not recognize ordinary coyote or dog predation of their animals. This argument doesn't hold water, however, since as the Cuero chupacabra case proves, ranchers can and do make mistakes, not only in claiming that chupacabra victims had been drained of blood, but also in identifying chupacabra carcasses themselves and correctly describing canid predation.

Scientific Analysis of Chupacabra Victims

Though relatively few chupacabra victims were examined by trained veterinarians or medical examiners, such an examination has occurred a few times, providing valuable insight into what science has to say about vampire victims. Dr. David Morales, a Puerto Rican veterinarian with the Department of Agriculture, conducted necropsies on hundreds of chupacabra victims from all across the island, every single one of which was claimed to have been mysteriously drained of blood. His results were revealed on the National Geographic TV show *Is It Real?* in 2005: "The man who spent the most time examining the chupacabra victims found that after 300 animal corpses, the rumor mill and the news reports had gotten it all wrong: the animals were *not* drained of blood and all had struggled violently against their attackers." That is, every single autopsy he conducted of the animals "without a drop of blood" had plenty of blood in them; there was no sign of any vampirism, and in fact they all showed signs of having been attacked by ordinary predators such as dogs, rhesus monkeys, and birds.

Morales was not alone in his analysis; other Puerto Rican veterinarians and medical experts who examined the alleged chupacabra victims came to the same conclusion. Dr. Hector J. Garcia, for example, head of the Agriculture Department's veterinary services, found that "the autopsies showed a variety of causes of death, including parasites. The animals that suffered bites, he said, more likely fell prey to the feral dogs that populate certain forests and rural areas. . . . All the dead animals, Dr. Garcia emphasized, had the expected amount of blood in them" (Navarro 1996).[1]

How Stories Begin

Jerry Ayer, the taxidermist who examined the Blanco chupacabra in 2009, offered his opinion of how these stories begin: "You live down here in south Texas, and you have a ranch or some livestock. Well, this animal is a predator— I know that because it's got canine teeth—and predators are usually nocturnal, they hunt at night. And this thing might come into your yard at night to take a chicken or a goat or whatever, and since it's a predator, it would go straight for the neck, and so by biting the neck it would leave two puncture wounds in the neck, and I can see how if the landowner heard the distressed livestock, he would go out to investigate. Well, at that point, the creature, whatever it is, would be scared away, it's not going to stand and bite if it's not in a corner. It would run off. So they would get this vague description of this dark hairless creature bounding off into the brush. And maybe upon inspection of the live-stock, they would see that their goat or their chicken would have two puncture wounds in the neck. I can see how many people would be quick to conclude that it's the rumored chupacabra, or start creating those stories" (Ayer 2009).

Mass Hysteria and the Chupacabra

There seems little doubt that there was a strong element of mass hysteria in most of the chupacabra sightings, and in Puerto Rico in particular. It's easy to scoff at the idea of mass hysteria (medically known as mass psychogenic ill-ness), and indeed denial is a common hallmark of mass hysteria. Those who are engaging in mass hysteria often reject the diagnosis, but that doesn't make it any less real. Others, when they hear or read the phrase *mass hysteria* think of a collective panic of drooling, mindless angry mobs burning down houses in search of witches. But mass hysterias are often far more subtle than that, may only involve a few dozen people, and last anywhere from hours to weeks. (For my investigations into some famous cases of mass hysteria, see my books *Scientific Paranormal Investigation: How to Solve Unexplained Mysteries* and *Hoaxes, Myths, and Manias: Why We Need Critical Thinking*.)

Mass hysteria is often fueled by the mass media; people read about scary things in the newspaper, or see televised reports on them, and concern about them spreads from person to person. I previously discussed the sensation-alized, alarmist news coverage that chupacabra reports generated within Puerto Rico, but the global news media helped spread it worldwide. As Loren Coleman and others have noted, the chupacabra did not really explode onto the global stage until March 1996, when the subject "appeared on the TV talk show *Christina* [sic], the Spanish-language Univision network's popu-lar counterpart to Oprah Winfrey. The media attention from this exposure appears to have caused the migration of Chupamania into Mexico and the United States" (Coleman 1999). The broadcast almost immediately spurred a sharp increase in reports from Mexico, Latin America, and Spanish-speaking areas of the United States.

Indeed, this sudden increase is very strong evidence for a cultural explanation, and fits perfectly as an example of mass hysteria. Unless the chupacabra animals watched the *Cristina* talk show (or somehow knew that the public's knowledge of their existence had skyrocketed outside of Puerto Rico) and they suddenly decided to move into areas where *Cristina* aired, there's no logical reason the creatures would suddenly begin being reported there. This same pattern can be found in the sighting reports of many other unknown monsters. For example, the number of sightings of lake monsters Ogopogo and Champ jumped dramatically following media publicity of the monsters, not following other sightings of the monsters. The most likely explanation is not that the creatures were suddenly more likely to be sighted because a newspaper story was published or TV show aired, but instead that people were more aware of the creatures, were expecting to see them, and interpreted any unusual event or sighting as the monster they had just heard about: ("Miguel! I just saw something weird in the woods as I drove home . . . I saw the news last week about *el chupacabra*—do you think it could have been that?"). Indeed, the "Chupamania" that Coleman refers to has nothing to do with any real creatures and everything to do with the *idea* of them. Therefore the "chupacabra reports" that appeared in the wake of the *Cristina* publicity were far more likely to be misunderstandings, misperceptions, and figments of the public's imagination and suggestion than any actual mysterious vampire creature. (For more on this topic, see page 134 of *Lake Monster Mysteries: Investigating the World's Most Elusive Creatures* [Radford and Nickell 2007].)

The situation got so bad in Mexico City in May 1996 that

parents in villages nationwide say they've been keeping their children home at night. It was against that backdrop that Abigael Carlos Tobon, a 25-year-old nurse, fell down the stairs . . . in this rural hamlet just outside Mexico City. By then, it seems, everyone—her neighbors, her mother, even the national media—was ready to believe almost anything. The story the following day would read that the goat-sucker had struck in Naucalpan and was closing in on the Mexican capital. "She was on the stairs, and she bent down like this," Abigael's brother, José, 24, explained on a treacherous, concrete stairway inside the family home. "She fell against the wall. The bone popped out of her arm, and she was screaming, 'Mama, I fell!' Because of all the rumors and news stories about the animal, my mother heard, 'Mama, animal!' and she started yelling that the chupacabra had gotten my sister. The arm was terribly broken—it looked like some animal had bitten it off." And when the neighbors ran in, José said, all they saw was the arm and, at that very moment, a black, winged mass—it turned out to be a flock of swallows—flying away through the dusk. "And that's how the rumor started here," he recalled. Even well-educated Mexicans like José—a graduate student in civil engineering at the capital's National Autonomous University of Mexico—are vulnerable right now to legends like that of the goatsucker. "I think yes, it exists," José maintained. "It just didn't attack my sister." (Fineman 1996)

This chupacabra report is a classic example of mass hysteria, where people's expectations guide their perceptions. Amid the fear and hysteria, a young woman's call "I fell" was interpreted as a warning call about an "animal"—not just any animal, but the chupacabra. An injury caused by a fall looked—for the moment anyway—like a chupacabra bite, and a flock of birds was seen as a scary, suspicious dark form flying into the night. Examples like this were not unusual in areas where chupacabra stories and rumors circulated, and with fearful people expecting to see scary and mysterious creatures at every turn, it's not surprising that chupacabra reports would surface.

In chapter 2 I briefly mentioned a chupacabra-like incident in 1974 Nebraska and South Dakota. I'll return to the case and reveal its eventual outcome, for it will by now be familiar. There are several precedents for a mass hysteria or collective delusion regarding mysterious animal killings. One of the best-known and best-researched examples occurred in the fall of 1974. Dead cattle were discovered with parts of their anatomy missing and mysterious blood loss (Stewart 1977). At around the same time, eyewitness sightings of UFOs and "a monster-thing" surfaced, presumably having attacked the cattle and drained their blood. The thing "was described by the few persons who allegedly observed it as a hairy creature that walked on all fours and quickly vanished when seen by humans. All sightings took place at night and not one actually got a good look at the animal."

Rumors spread among the rural community, and in a close parallel to the situation in Puerto Rico, the news media reported each new dead animal discovery with sensationalism and alarm. "During the peak of the episode, radio and television broadcasts and newspapers contained daily accounts of newly discovered mutilations. In addition media coverage generally contained interviews with law enforcement officials, veterinarians, or other knowledgeable persons. These interviews often confounded rather than elucidated the search for the cause of the mutilations and frequently contained unsupported personal opinions."

Details that could have been directly lifted from 1995 Canovanas, Puerto Rico, chupacabra reports appeared: animals were drained of blood by a predator that left no tracks or footprints. Farmers insisted that their cattle had been mysteriously killed by some unknown attacker, possibly extraterrestrials, Satanists, or the elusive "monster-thing." However, "The reports of the two state veterinary-diagnostic laboratories stated that every animal brought to them had died of natural causes and that predators, by tearing away the soft parts of the carcass, had been responsible for the apparent 'mutilations.'" They also explained the apparently blood-drained bodies: "veterinarians pointed out that after a few days the blood of dead animals coagulates and gives the impression that the body has been drained."

At the end of this episode, every supposedly mysterious detail of the bloodsucking "monster-thing" and its victims was explained. Stewart concludes that "[t]his episode appears to be a classic case of mild mass hysteria" in which "for inexplicable reasons people suddenly perceive the mundane in a new, bizarre fashion . . . Everyday occurrences are given a new, exciting, anxiety-producing definition."

And what of the chupacabra-like "man-thing" seen only in glimpses, which had presumably preyed on the cattle's blood? No sign of it was ever found—no tracks or traces of it at all. It was never photographed, nor actually seen sucking blood. Other than a few glimpses of something odd in the dark of night, there was no evidence it ever existed. Imagination and suggestion can easily account for those reports.

All in all, this report from the heartland of America in 1974 is virtually identical to chupacabra reports from Puerto Rico in 1995. The main difference is that in 1974, the natural explanations for the supposedly mysterious cattle deaths and vampirism were eventually accepted by the community. If the events of 1974 occurred today—especially in Texas or the American Southwest—it is certain that the chupacabra would be blamed, and perhaps even reported or "sighted."

Dr. David Morales, the Puerto Rican veterinarian with the Department of Agriculture mentioned earlier, believes that mass hysteria was clearly at work on his home island: "I think what went on in Puerto Rico from 1994 to 1996 was a mass hysteria. Someone made up the name chupacabra and from that moment on, every animal that died was the result of the chupacabra" (*Is It Real?* 2005).

The Chupacabra as a Zoological Reality

So far I have examined every claim and piece of evidence for the chupacabra, and found all of them wanting. It was a good, if exhausting, exercise in clearly and carefully analyzing claims. Perhaps one of the most remarkable aspects of the chupacabra is the notoriety it gained during the past fifteen years despite a lack of good evidence.

The idea of thousands, or tens of thousands, of chupacabras existing somewhere out there without leaving far better traces of their presence beggars belief. If chupacabras exist, where are all their victims? Unverified reports of blood-drained livestock are very rare, a few per year at most. Presumably chupacabras must eat and suck blood every day (and a lot of it, for a four-to-five-foot creature). And there cannot be only one chupacabra, there must be large populations of them to keep the species alive, hundreds or thousands of them. That's a lot of blood; where are they getting it all? From a few chickens or goats every few months (that are in fact not actually missing any blood)?

It is also interesting to note that the chupacabras have never killed a human, unlike every other animal known to be predatory, including dogs, coyotes, and bobcats. Why would that be? Surely an animal as powerful and fearsome as a chupacabra, which has supposedly taken down thousands of animals including healthy cattle, could easily kill a person. Yet it doesn't happen—perhaps for the same reason that we don't hear news reports of manticore mutilations and lynchings by leprechauns.

While we are wondering about where all the dead bodies are, what about all the footprints? One of the most remarkable things about the chupacabra is its ability to avoid leaving footprints. Writer Marc Davenport puzzled over the lack of footprints: "Despite numerous face-to-face sightings of the animal standing on the ground and the documented killing of hundreds of animals, I know of no footprints known to have been left by the creature. I personally crawled through the back yards of witnesses on my hands and knees and questioned numerous others without finding anything but dog, goat, and chicken prints, and shoe marks." Since the time that Davenport was writing, there have been a few (very few) alleged footprints left by the creatures. But his point about the extreme scarcity of footprints is quite valid: "Unless the animal has some kind of wide, pillow-like structures on the bottom of its feet—which none of the witnesses have reported—it should leave footprints" (quoted in Corrales 1997, 5).

There are perhaps a half-dozen (alleged) footprints in existence, each more dubious than the last. Yet there have been hundreds of chupacabra reports—in fact some sightings involving multiple creatures. Just for the sake of argument, let's say that there have been two hundred chupacabra reports of varying credibility, and that half of them report a bipedal creature, and the other half report a quadruped animal. Assuming decent soil in which to capture prints, that would mean that we might potentially expect to find six hundred unique footprints or tracks in those sightings. Since virtually every report involves the chupacabra moving (if the animal simply stood still, we'd expect to have much better descriptions, if not photographs), the number of footprints we'd expect to see doubles with every step it takes. There should be tens of thousands of chupacabra tracks from those two hundred sighted chupacabras alone—to say nothing of the chupacabras that presumably exist but are *not* seen or reported. Including those chupacabras, we might expect to see hundreds of thousands of chupacabra prints. Yet we only have a paltry half-dozen or so alleged tracks, a tiny fraction of 1 percent of what we might find. What sort of creatures leaves virtually no footprints? Nonexistent ones.

Every single case of an alleged chupacabra victim or carcass has failed to yield any hard evidence. Outside of carnival sideshows, there are no chupacabra teeth, bones, bodies, hair, or anything else. There are some alleged footprints and photos, but most are jokes and hoaxes—nothing that has been carefully or scientifically analyzed.

Is it possible that chupacabras really do exist, and are sleeping in caves or sucking the blood out of hapless chickens as you read these words? Certainly, anything is *possible*. The question is not what is possible, but what the evidence and logic show. In the case of the chupacabra, the closer you examine the mystery, the less evidence there is. Every time an animal claimed to be a chupacabra has been scientifically analyzed, it has been identified as a known animal. When hard evidence is available, we find an explanation.

Folklore of the Chupacabra

As I noted in chapter 2, vampire elements are among the most common folklore motifs worldwide. From Asia to Africa to South America, there are stories of strange animals that prey on animals and people. In South America, they have an entity called the *likichiri*, which steals blood and fat from native people. In South Africa, witches are said to kill people and take their blood and body parts. In Europe, of course, there were many vampire tales, and they arose in a similar manner to that of the chupacabra: people trying to explain things they didn't understand, such as the reason for bad fortune, crop failures, and livestock deaths. It is also important to remember that while a few dead goats or cattle or other livestock may not seem that important, for many poor farmers that loss can be severe.

The chupacabra is best understood from the point of view of folklore or cultural tradition; it is impossible to take seriously as an account of a real, biological creature. For example, it is odd that the chupacabra is reported almost exclusively in Spanish-speaking areas. (The Maine monster is an exception, though chupacabra was only one of several proposed explanations.) There is no other animal that exists only where a particular language is spoken. Livestock are kept by ranchers and farmers all over the world, yet the chupacabra only attacks the cattle and goats of people who speak Spanish (or associate with those who do). This fact makes even less sense when you geographically map the spread of chupacabra reports. How is it that, if the chupacabra is a real creature, it somehow swam or flew nearly four thousand miles from Puerto Rico to Spain yet never managed to get to Haiti, which is only three hundred miles away—and where French is spoken?

Furthermore, livestock predation only really makes the news when a chupacabra is suspected. But these things happen all the time—ranchers complain about wild dogs and even wolves coming in from Yellowstone National Park, for example. Those ranchers don't assume that the chupacabra is attacking their animals, because it's not a part of their culture, and because they have seen dogs and wolves attack cattle.

While for many the chupacabra is a harmless joke or a curiosity, there is real danger for the many others who take it seriously. Daniel Altschuler, a Puerto Rican scientist formerly at the Arecibo Radio Observatory, cautions that there is some danger in continuing to employ the chupacabra as an explanation: "In the case of the chupacabra, as entertaining as it might be, it might lead people—and it does lead people—to confuse reality and fiction. An explanation that isn't an explanation is dangerous because it might lead people not to really find the truth" (Altschuler 2005). In other words, if a rancher concludes that the legendary chupacabra killed his livestock, that prevents him from finding out what *really* attacked his animals. If the rancher is falsely confident that his animals were not attacked by some known predator (or disease, or another natural phenomenon), then he will not take steps to prevent future attacks. It is important to find the real culprit, for the same reason that police should not stop looking for a missing person if someone suggests that the person may have been abducted by a UFO.

Early reports of chupacabras simply described a small, fearsome creature that attacked small animals. Interestingly, chupacabra descriptions grew wilder and more exaggerated the farther they got from Puerto Rico. Reports from South America and Spain claimed some animals sprouted wings on their backs, some had red eyes, and others kangaroo-like legs. Such claims are a classic sign of folklore, and are hard to explain if what is described is a real creature. After all, kangaroos don't grow wings when they are seen outside of Australia, and polar bears don't sport zebra stripes away from the Arctic. As we have seen, just about any strange creature, from an ocean skate to a coyote, can be identified as a chupacabra. The chupacabra label was simply a catch-all name for "something strange I can't identify." This attribution often happens in monster sightings, where any phenomenon that seems odd or inexplicable is "identified" as Bigfoot, or a lake monster, or a chupacabra. As Jonathan Downes, author of *Island of Paradise*, notes, "the word chupacabra has become very misused . . . the word chupacabra means boogeyman, monster, spectre, ghoul—and it means that all around the Spanish-speaking world" (Downes 2008b).

The Chupacabra, Like All Vampires, Is Immortal

One may be forgiven for wondering, given the huge gaps in logic and good evidence, why many people around the world believe in the chupacabra. Though this is the first book to take an in-depth, critical examination of the phenomenon, there were surely enough red flags to alert people that the story simply does not hold together. There are several reason why it has taken so long for this mystery to be solved.

Sloppy Research

One of the most important reasons the mystery has lasted more than a decade and a half is that it was never really investigated properly. Over and over, more often than not, so-called researchers failed to conduct anything resembling a close, careful investigation of the facts. Eyewitnesses were not questioned to corroborate evidence. Bald, often self-contradictory assertions were accepted uncritically and taken at face value. Leads were rarely followed up, and when they were, the questions were cursory.

In his *Chupacabras* book, Scott Corrales provides an excellent example of the anemic level of analysis, investigation, and expertise typically brought to bear on chupacabra incidents. José Miguel Agosto, the husband of Madelyne Tolentino, described the bite marks he believed were left by the chupacabra:

"Surgical cuts. Perfect ones. If they were made by an animal or wild dogs, they would tear the flesh, but no, these are perfect cuts, as if made by a scalpel. . . . In some cases it has taken the animals' genitals. It apparently rips them out and takes them since they are nowhere to be found. It has taken their livers and other body parts" (Corrales 1997, 47).

Agosto related another attack, this one on sheep in the Canovanas neighborhood of Quebrada Prieta. "There was no blood on the wound, nor on the ground." When asked to clarify by the interviewer, Agosto contradicted himself when he said there was no blood: "It sometimes leaves them with some blood. The strange thing is that when it leaves them with some blood, it won't flow. The blood remains in the body" (Corrales 1997, 49). He added, "The sheep had been dead for a day or more, and they were still flexible—not stiff at all. These are things that make you think [how mysterious it is] . . . It's as if the creature [chupacabra] gave them a liquid that kept them entirely flexible. . . . Remember that when an animal decomposes, the worms appear right away, and there were no worms, either."

From such comments, it is clear that Agosto's medical and forensic knowledge is virtually nonexistent, and what he does know is mostly wrong. He is baffled by several perfectly natural and normal decomposition processes, confidently and prematurely proclaiming a mystery where none exists. He finds the fact that sheep were flexible to be a genuine mystery, assuming that the animals would be stiff as a board because of the dying muscles contracting into rigor mortis. But Agosto seems unaware that rigor mortis is a temporary condition, and passes after several hours (depending on many conditions including the temperature, humidity, etc.; Cunliffe 2009). It would not be at all unusual to find dead animals that were very flexible.

Furthermore, his opinion that worms appear in wounds or flesh immediately after an animal dies is completely wrong. According to Dr. Clare Cunliffe (2009), the forensic pathologist and medical examiner, "it would take them a day or so at least" to appear. His claim that bites by animals or wild dogs "would tear the flesh" is simply not true, and easily disproven by doing a quick web search for photographs of dog bites. Most dog bites are simple puncture wounds created by the canine teeth, and do not necessarily rip the flesh at all. And so on. However sincere and well-meaning Agosto is, he is completely ignorant of the forensic processes he is speaking about. The mysteries he sees (and that Scott Corrales reports) are not the result of any unexplained phenomenon, but instead his own lack of expertise and knowledge.

Unfortunately, most people who write books on mysterious animals and the unexplained are authors, not investigators. They have no background or training in investigation, and see their role as merely collecting and reporting these unusual sightings. While collecting and reporting serve an important function, these mysteries, to be understood, must be carefully and critically examined. A true investigator is not content to simply report without analysis.

Chupacabra and Conspiracies

A second reason for the longevity of the chupacabra story lies in the nature of what people believe the chupacabra to be. Whether the result of a top-secret U.S. government genetics experiment or an extraterrestrial, most explanations of the chupacabra share a common theme: conspiracy. The chupacabra is unique in this regard; Bigfoot and the Loch Ness monster are not the subject of claimed conspiracies by the U.S. government.

Chupacabra lore is rife with conspiracy theory: in Puerto Rico the creature was likely an escaped beast that would make Dr. Moreau proud; in Chile the government conspired with NASA and the American military to "weaponize" chupacabras; in Nicaragua the university professionals secretly switched Mr. Talavera's real chupacabra carcass for that of a dog. And so on; in each case the skeptical experts, professionals, and investigators are dismissed while the chupacabra lumbers on. I expect that any true believers in the chupacabra who are reading this book (if they have gotten this far) will assume I am part of the conspiracy as well, that I have some financial or ideological motive for trying to debunk this vampire.

Little wonder, then, that the occasional attempts by governmental officials to quell fears and calm citizens are often met with dismissals and jeers. One of the hallmarks of conspiracy theories is that they cannot be effectively disproven; any evidence that negates or undermines the theory is itself part of the conspiracy. For those who are certain that the chupacabra exists, no amount of evidence or arguments will prove to them otherwise. There will always be explanations they refuse to accept, preferring fanciful fables over simple scientific truths.

Conclusions

Let us return to the account that began this book and spurred my five-year investigation into the chupacabra, that of vampire Peter Plogojowitz. In his case we see a very familiar pattern of vampirism claims, including being blamed for causing the deaths of nine people and having sucked blood from them. Though there was never any real evidence or logical link between the mysterious deaths and vampirism (or Plogojowitz, for that matter), the connection was clear and obvious in many people's minds.

The pattern is repeated with remarkable regularity in the history of the bloodsucking vampire chupacabra. Like the European vampires, the chupacabra claims usually begin with one or more unexplained, mysterious deaths and the search for a culprit. Also like the European vampires, the chupacabra is said to suck blood, usually by night—and it is rarely if ever caught in the act; it is only in the cold light of morning that their bloody signature handiwork is seen. Revenant vampires, like the chupacabra, have never been photographed, nor even proven to exist. The parallels go on and on. The chupacabra is merely a recent incarnation of a centuries-old vampire myth, with a Hispanic twist.

For this reason alone, the chupacabra will live on. People will still glimpse odd animals in the inky darkness and call it the goatsucker. Dead animals will still be found mysteriously "without a drop of blood" in them by panicked ranchers and farmers who don't think (or don't bother) to have the carcasses examined by knowledgeable experts to verify vampirism. Mangy dogs and coyotes will still be found and (for a period of weeks or months between discovery and DNA analysis) briefly called the elusive chupacabra.

Why, then, write this book? Why spend considerable time, effort, and money to disprove something that skeptics never believed existed in the first place, and which believers will ignore? There are two answers. The first is that this book was written for people with open minds, not those closed with certainty on either end of the spectrum. I've done my best to research, understand, and explain the entire chupacabra phenomenon using logic and scientific analysis, and ultimately readers will make up their own minds.

The more important answer is that my research is not really about the chupacabra, for the vampiric beast almost certainly cannot and does not exist. This book is about folklore made "real," about how ancient superstitions inherent in the human mind gave the European vampire a fearsome new face at the end of the twentieth century. It is about how sincere, respected eyewitnesses who claim to have seen monsters can be completely wrong. It is about how careful investigation and science can solve mysteries created by rumor, speculation, and sloppy research. It is about how rumor combined with sensationalized news reports helped create a monster, and about how the chupacabra label fills the gap between what laypeople guess and what scientists know.

As I have shown, the chupacabra is unnecessary; it is antiquated and obsolete. It served its purpose and should be put out to pasture (where it would no doubt prefer to be anyway). Like its vampire forefathers, the chupacabra was created as an "explanation" for things people did not understand: strange monster sightings, "mysterious" animal deaths, apparent blood loss, and so on. We have scientific, credible answers to every single one of these mysteries; there is no need to conjure the bloodthirsty beast, except perhaps as a lesson in human psychology and fallibility.

I have shown that the popular image of the chupacabra—the one appearing on hundreds of books, magazines, and websites as a credible eyewitness description—is in fact based on an alien creature in a science fiction film. The eyewitness sighting that produced that description is riddled with implausibilities, and later "eyewitnesses" who confirmed that sighting could not have been correct. News reports of the time about the beast contained both exaggeration and outright misinformation, which was often regurgitated as gospel truth by later writers less interested in facts than in a bone-cracking good story.

In the years after the creature's appearance in 1995, the word *chupacabra* lost whatever original meaning it had, and became a word for a Hispanic boogeyman and a catch-all pop culture term for any strange animal seen or found—with or without any connection to bloodless prey. A dozen or so mangy dogs and coyotes appeared in the American Southwest, temporarily called chupacabras until one by one experts and DNA analysis identified and classified them.

And all along, the stories of vampirism were elevated from rumor, assumption, and speculation to verified fact through sensational tabloid reports and sloppy research. There is no credible scientific evidence that any animals were mysteriously drained of blood, and strong evidence that they were not.

To believe that the chupacabra exists is to believe that tens of thousands of large, bipedal unknown bloodsucking beasts with the characteristics of a dozen different animals suddenly and mysteriously appeared in 1995 Puerto Rico, and have been attacking livestock in a dozen different countries for the past fifteen years, without leaving a single dead body, bone, or tooth, or even a single credible footprint.

The original Puerto Rican chupacabra has been completely discredited by a close look at the cultural context, claims, and eyewitness accounts. The North and Latin American chupacabras have been discredited by logic, science, and DNA testing. There is nothing left to explain, no place left for any mystery to hide. The beast is gone—in fact never was—but the myth will continue. The chupacabra is dead. Long live the chupacabra.

Comparison of Ten Notable Chupacabra Reports, 1995–2010

Location	Finder/ Witness/ Owner	Date	Photo	Carcass	Vampirism Claimed	Scientific Analysis/ DNA Results
Canovanas, Puerto Rico	M. Tolentino	August 1995	No	No	No	N/A
Malpaisillo, Nicaragua	J. Talavera	August 2000	No	Skeleton	Yes	Dog
Rio Rancho, New Mexico	B. Wheeler	2002 (reported 2005)	Yes	Yes	No	Skate
Turner, Maine	M. O'Donnell	August 2006	Yes	Yes	No	Dog
Albuquerque, New Mexico	W. Kalberg	September 2007	Yes	No	No	N/A (identified as dog)
Cuero, Texas	P. Canion	July 2007	Yes	Yes	Yes	Coyote
Blanco, Texas	J. Ayer	July 2009	Yes	Yes	No	Not done (suspected coyote)
Elmendorf, Texas	D. McAnally	May 2004	Yes	Yes	No	Dog
Wise County, Texas	T. Potter	January 2010	Yes	Yes	No	Raccoon
Horizon City, Texas	C. Garcia	January 2010	No	No	No	N/A

Comparison of the ten most notable chupacabra reports, focusing on those in which a carcass was recovered for analysis. Note that 80 percent of the cases do not involve claims of blood sucked from animals, and that the animal was identified in every case where scientific analysis was conducted.

Appendix 2

How to Identify a Chupacabra

Since the true nature of the chupacabra, if it exists, is unknown, there is of course no way to conclusively identify an animal as a chupacabra. However, there are scientific ways to tell whether or not a given live or dead animal *could possibly* be an alleged chupacabra, based on their reputed characteristics. This list, derived from a close analysis of alleged chupacabra discoveries, will help future farmers, ranchers, and others who find an unusual animal to decide whether or not their animal could be a chupacabra.

1. Was the animal actually seen attacking other animals?
2. If it was, was it seen or videotaped sucking blood from its victim(s)?
3. Was a suspected chupacabra victim autopsied by a qualified veterinarian or medical pathologist?
4. Did this veterinarian or pathologist conclude that blood had actually been extracted from the animal?
5. Does the suspected chupacabra have a mouth structure that would allow it to physically suck out the blood of its prey?
6. Has the suspected chupacabra's saliva been scientifically tested for the specific anticoagulant and anesthetic properties it must have to suck blood?
7. Has the suspected chupacabra's digestive and intestinal tract been examined for specialized structures or enzymes that would suggest it could live on a diet of blood without succumbing to iron toxicity?
8. Have the suspected chupacabra's stomach contents been examined to determine if it lived on a diet of blood (instead of ordinary canid prey)?
9. Have samples of the suspected chupacabra been subjected to DNA sequencing?
10. Has scientific testing of samples of the suspected chupacabra's skin conclusively ruled out sarcoptic mange or another skin disease?

These are basic scientific questions that must be addressed if a suspected chupacabra specimen is to be taken seriously by anyone other than ill-informed monster enthusiasts and chupacabra promoters. Most of these issues require analysis by knowledgeable medical or veterinary personnel. After all, the identification of an animal—any animal, even one that may not exist—is ultimately an issue for zoological science. While these examinations and tests may run a few hundred dollars, it's a small price to pay if the creature actually is the world's first authenticated chupacabra. Unfortunately, in the dozen or so cases of found "chupacabra" carcasses, few of these questions have even been asked, much less answered.

Appendix 3

2010 *Interview with Madelyne Tolentino*

In 2010 during final preparation for this book, I renewed my efforts to interview Madelyne Tolentino, the most famous and influential chupacabra eyewitness in history. Tolentino was interviewed a few months after her sighting (a transcript of which is available online—see Plá 1996—and in Scott Corrales's book *Chupacabras and Other Mysteries*). Tolentino's version of events has changed somewhat over the past fifteen years, as one would expect from any eyewitness. A detailed analysis of her sighting is beyond the scope of this section, but my interview with her produced some interesting revelations.

Tolentino's sighting occurred at some point during the second week of August 1995 at about one o'clock in the afternoon. She doesn't recall the date, but said that it was a weekday, which would place it between August 7 and 11. She said the sighting lasted from three to five minutes (though it's important to note that eyewitnesses often greatly overestimate the duration of their experiences; time seems to "slow down" when witnesses are excited or startled, and seconds can seem like minutes). Though it happened near a fairly busy road, during that time no other cars appeared.

Only she and her mother saw the creature. Tolentino was sleeping, and her mother woke her up with shouting, saying she'd seen some animal outside. They both looked through a window to the street outside. "My mother said, 'I'm going to grab it,' and she opened the door and started to go out. I asked my mother, 'How are [you] so brave?'" Her mother did not leave the house, but the pair watched it as it stood outside a window for a while, then floated (or hopped) toward tall grass in a vacant lot across the street; then it disappeared. In an interview published in *Chupacabras and Other Mysteries*, Tolentino is quoted as saying that a young boy who worked for her then-husband chased the animal down and opened its mouth, but she told me that never happened: "José had a young worker who used to help him fix cars, and he ran out to see, but he did not see the chupacabra."

Tolentino corrected several mistakes in the famous drawing based on her sighting. For example, the creature was about three feet tall (not four to five, as had been reported). It did not have claws but instead "[i]t had human hands—not claws but long fingers and human-like nails. Its eyes were big and *achiandos* [Chinese-slanty], and it didn't have a nose, just two little dots. The creature's skin was not brown but grayish . . . it looked like leather, wet and wrinkled. Its skin was like an extraterrestrial—but I never said it was an extraterrestrial. I have an interest in UFOs and aliens, but I never said it was either an extraterrestrial or an animal. I don't know what it was. I've never changed my story," she told me. "The whole experience seemed both real and unreal at the same time.

"It was not bald, it did have some hair on it. In a few places it had rough patches, like it was burned." At one point she stooped down to see if there were any sexual parts on the creature, "But it was 'plain,' there was nothing there at all. And the hair was short, so I would have seen if there had been any type of genitalia. This made me think it was not of this world." She also reported smelling sulfur at the time. I asked her how it moved: "It was skipping like a kangaroo, but it had no tail. It did not touch the ground . . . it had no wings, but it came out like it was running as it approached." (I asked Tolentino how it could be *both* skipping *and* not touching the ground, but did not get a clarifying answer.)

Tolentino said that she encountered the chupacabra a second time, in December of that year when she and her son were in a taxi on their way to a store to pick up a layaway Christmas gift. She did not actually see the creature, but inferred its presence because she smelled sulfur: "'It is here,' I said to myself." She has not seen it since.

Notes

Chapter 1

1. Note on the spelling of *chupacabra*: Some researchers insist that the correct Spanish spelling of the goatsucker is *chupacabras*. Others, however, disagree. As one researcher noted, the name *chupacabras* is "[i]ncorrectly pluralized, its name evokes the speech of the lower classes in the Hispanic Caribbean who are prone to eliminate the 's' form from everyday speech, but then tend to hypercorrect pluralization in the presence of interlocutors especially status superiors, sprinkling s's in their speech indiscriminately" (Derby 2008, 298). While many native Spanish speakers do indeed use *chupacabras*, others use *chupacabra*. Because *chupacabra* is the most common spelling, I will use that for the singular form throughout the book.

2. In 2010 a filmmaker named Paul Kimball released parts of a documentary titled *Island of Blood*. The piece followed researcher Nick Redfern and others as they visited Puerto Rico in search of the chupacabra. Loren Coleman of the website Cryptomundo.com asked me to comment on three short clips of the film, and here I provide a short analysis of some of the investigational shortcomings. Redfern is told about an alleged chupacabra attack in which sixty-five pigs were mysteriously killed in a local prison. Redfern follows up with, "Were they attacked like the classic chupacabra attack?" His informant, Mr. Pla, replies, "They had a hole, a perforation in the armpit." Redfern then asks, "In every one?" Pla states, "In every one." That concludes the exchange, and Redfern seems to be satisfied with the answer he got. But he doesn't seem to notice that his question was never really answered; in fact, if anything, the answer he got suggests it was *not* a chupacabra attack!

    The main characteristic of a "classic chupacabra attack" is a loss of blood; a secondary typical characteristic is puncture marks on the victim's neck. Not only was there no mention of bloodsucking, but the marks were on the shoulder or armpit instead of the neck. It is baffling that neither of the two "classic" characteristics of the chupacabra attack was mentioned in this case (or at least in the parts presented in the video), yet Redfern doesn't comment on this inconsistency and instead asks if "every one" of the pigs died that way.

    Either he's *assuming* that the pigs were drained of blood, or he was told this off-camera, or for some reason he doesn't notice that the answer to his question was basically, "No, the pig attacks were not like the classic chupacabra attack." Redfern seems to simply assume that what he's being told is valid and accurate, without doing any research or investigation to confirm it. This case is presented as evidence of a chupacabra attack, but it's all anecdote. There's no follow-up, no eyewitnesses interviewed, no nothing.

In another section, Redfern hears one man's story that "men in black" government agents showed up at a rural farm following an incident in which a machete had been broken supposedly while fending off a chupacabra. These men confiscated the broken machete and took it away, presumably to hide evidence. Redfern seems to accept this wild conspiracy story without a shred of evidence other than one man's story, commenting, "That might suggest that whoever they were, they knew where this creature was that night and a good idea where it had attacked, and what it had attacked." Again, no effort whatsoever is made to confirm any details, seek any other eyewitnesses, or anything else.

To be fair, Redfern later clarified that the sections that were posted online were footage shot for another film called *Fields of Fear*, and not really intended to be a fleshed-out, comprehensive documentary on the chupacabra. Still, the sections that were posted suggest that the investigation was perhaps not as critical or thorough as it could have been.

Chapter 2

1. Though the vampire is known in one form or another worldwide, often those who believe in the local variants will deny that they believe in vampires. It's a case of how one man's religion is another man's superstition: As Matthew Beresford notes in his book *From Demons to Dracula*, "'Vampire' is merely the English variant of a much wider collection of terms denoting variants of the mythical being: in Romania the terms *moroi, strigoi*, and *pricolici* are used . . . In the West, Romania is deemed by many to be the home of the vampire and yet Romanians themselves believe there are no vampires there at all; rather . . . they believe that Romania is the home of supernatural beings such as the aforementioned *strigoi*" (Beresford 2008, 8). Indeed, people I interviewed in La Paz, Bolivia, about the Andean vampire *likichiri* asserted that though vampires were mythical, the *likichiri* was very much real. In the same way, many Puerto Ricans would probably dismiss vampires as mere fiction while accepting the existence of the bloodsucking chupacabra.

2. The Andean vampires became the subject of a bizarre international news story at the end of 2009, when four Peruvians were arrested on suspicion of killing dozens of people in order to extract their fat and tissues for cosmetic uses in Europe. According to one BBC News (2009) story, "The gang allegedly targeted people on remote roads, luring them with fake job offers before killing them and extracting their fat. The liquidized product fetched $15,000 a liter and police suspect it was sold on to companies in Europe. . . . Police said the gang could be behind the disappearances of up to 60 people in Peru's Huanuco and Pasco regions. One of those arrested told police the ringleader had been killing people for their fat for more than three decades." The police even displayed bottles of the seized fat for the press and public upon making the announcement. An international outcry arose, and the vampiric fat-stealing gang bust was soon exposed as a hoax. There were in fact some murders—but they were committed by corrupt police officers using the ancient vampire myth as a cover-up for their real crimes.

3. Puerto Rican researcher Lucas Montes, whose hometown is very near Moca, told me that "*El vampiro de Moca* was a totally different incident not related at all to the chupacabra. Some researchers want to link both incidents as being of the same origin, but that is totally wrong. I did some research and found out that there were humans involved in killing animals just to see their antics in the newspaper" (Montes 2010). Due to time constraints I was unable to investigate this claim personally while in Puerto Rico, but faking a "mysterious" chupacabra-like attack (especially one without confirmed blood loss) would not be difficult. A hoaxer would merely need to poison an animal (or break its neck), then create two puncture wounds with a nail or screwdriver.

Chapter 3

1. I have encountered this exaggeration of the public's fear many times in my investigations into mysterious creatures. For example, in 2007 when I investigated the popobawa—a skeptic-raping bat-demon-vampire-ghost reported on the East African island of Zanzibar—in my initial research I often found references suggesting that belief in the popobawa's existence was widespread. Yet when I actually investigated firsthand, I found that exactly the opposite was true. A local researcher and I spent hours looking for anyone who believed that the creature was real instead of a myth. Dozens of people dismissed the popobawa as a joke or an urban legend, though I did eventually find a few people who believed in its existence (Radford 2008).

Chapter 5

1. According to Mr. McAnally, there were actually at least three separate DNA analyses on his Elmendorf beast (McAnally 2009b). Dr. Disotell's analysis, mentioned in the text, was the third and only completed analysis. The first, between August 2004 and January 2005, was "financed by Communion, parent corporation of the radio program *Coast to Coast*, and analyzed by the University of California-Davis. . . . The results were inconclusive due to 'overexposure to extreme heat or radioactive material.'" McAnally claims that Whitley Strieber, of Communion, had violated their agreement, and that he never received the promised DNA report. The second, conducted between March 2006 and January 2007, was conducted by a production company under assignment from Disney Studios. That analysis was never completed, but preliminary testing suggested it might be coyote. More details can be found at McAnally's website, TexasBlueDog.org.

Chapter 6

1. Canion expanded on her thoughts about the University of Texas DNA analysis on her website, comparing herself to Theodore Roosevelt, noting that he too searched for unknown animals, and found one: "There was a myth for a thousand

years of a huge black and white demon beast with red glowing eyes that would rip a man to shreds if he ventured into its lair. This beast was elusive for a thousand years of tales, until one brave American set out to prove it existed—and he did!! The beast turned out to be the Giant Panda, and the man was none other that President Theodore Roosevelt (Teddy). So, let's not quickly dismiss the notion of a new species being identified" (Canion 2009).

We see a familiar scorn and defensiveness about scientists when Canion asks, "How can experts say we know all the mammals with absolute certainty?" But this is a fallacious straw man argument, for to the best of my knowledge not a single "expert" (and certainly no zoologist or scientist) ever stated that all mammals on earth had been discovered with absolute certainty. Science is always subject to revision and new knowledge and discoveries, and the idea of "absolute certainty" is itself not a scientific idea.

She takes this logical error even further, asking, "It is claimed that the chimpanzee genes have a 98% similarity to human genes, and this is promoted as evidence for the claim that apes are related to humans. Does this conclude that man is really equivalent to a monkey? I pose the question: Does the *almost* in the DNA sample make the unidentified beast (Chupacabra) equivalent to a coyote? Almost is not exact." It is true that humans and chimpanzees share about 95% of genetic material, but no one has ever suggested that it implies that a human is "equivalent" to a chimpanzee (whatever "equivalent" would mean in this context). Canion is simply blending a few nuggets of fact and truth, extrapolating them far beyond any logic or science, then "debunking" the myths that she herself made up.

2. In 2009 Canion found another chupacabra very similar in appearance to the first one. On her website she included a photograph titled "The Chupacabra Footprint," captioned, "Footprint does not match that of a coyote nor that of a wolf!" It's not clear where Canion got her information, but she is simply wrong; a comparison of Canion's photo with a published tracking guide (Wade and Bowns 1984, 41) reveals that the "chupacabra" track is identical to that of a coyote, down to the shape and placement of the toes and the claw marks.

Chapter 7

1. One woman I interviewed in Puerto Rico told me of a male friend of hers who often exhibited a flair for both drama and pranks, and now works in theater. Growing up near San Juan as a teenager during a time when UFOs and aliens were the subject of news and rumor, he would sometimes put on strange, makeshift costumes (such as wrapping himself in aluminum foil) and go out at night, riding his bicycle within sight of public roadways. After an hour or so of fun he would bike back to his house, ditch the costume, and eagerly wait to hear if any neighbors reported seeing anything strange. I was not able to confirm the story, but (having done similar teenage stunts myself) I have no reason to doubt it.

2. Without having access to the original Spanish-language interview done with Tolentino in 1996, it is impossible to know whether the details of her story have

actually changed over time, or if they were incorrectly reported (or mistranslated) in the first place. It is not unusual for important eyewitness stories and recollections to change over time (for an example involving Sandra Mansi's encounter with the Lake Champlain monster, see appendix 1 in my book *Lake Monster Mysteries*); on the other hand, given the poor scholarship rampant in chupacabra research, misreporting or mistranslating is also quite plausible.

3. Researcher Jonathan Downes provided some slime supposedly found on feathers taken from a chupacabra victim to the TV show *Proof Positive* in 1997; according to him, that analysis "showed nothing at all." In Scott Corrales's writings on the chupacabra there are multiple references to supposed recovered samples of the creature's fetid flesh, slime, and drool, yet all are mere myths.

4. A close analysis reveals why Jorge Martín's sketch of Tolentino's chupacabra is so inaccurate. The drawing, supposedly based on Tolentino's eyewitness account, is actually a combination of *several* eyewitness descriptions, including that of a man named Daniel Perez. Martín's mistake is clear: he assumed that Tolentino and Perez saw the same thing, and so he incorporated elements from both descriptions. This was an important logical mistake, because the sightings were completely independent of each other and in fact differed significantly. Martín missed the logical conclusion—that the eyewitnesses were seeing different things (regardless of what they were called)—and instead created a drawing of a largely (or completely) fictional hybrid that actually didn't end up matching any specific eyewitness descriptions. In essence, Martín decided to "average" out the reported features over several sightings, arbitrarily adding or dropping features or characteristics according to his personal whim or to what made a more interesting drawing. This averaging is completely unscientific, and demonstrates incompetence in the field of investigation (imagine if police detectives searching for suspects in two different crimes got one eyewitness description of a tall black male, and another of a short white male, and thus began looking for a mixed-race male of medium height and complexion). If a third eyewitness had claimed to have seen a strange creature with webbed duck feet, Martín would likely have incorporated that detail into his art as well. Yet his flawed sketch became the most famous and influential chupacabra depiction.

5. In the film *Species*, Sil is not, strictly speaking, a vampire. But it is certainly vampire-like, for in its quest to breed, it seeks out and extracts (with deadly consequences for the unlucky and unwitting "donor") not blood but semen. In her alluring human form (played by Natasha Henstridge), Sil sexually vampirizes several men she/it comes in contact with—much like the succubus of folklore.

6. As we can see from this exchange, Tolentino went far beyond simply stating that the film reminded her of real life in Puerto Rico. She was asked specifically and directly if the film made her "think there might have been an experiment in which a being escaped and is now at large"—clearly referring to contemporaneous (1995–1996) real-life Puerto Rico—and her answer was yes. Furthermore, she states that she had heard from a journalist whom she considers credible ("he knows a lot about it") that some unknown "experimental" creature had escaped from Puerto

Rico's El Yunque forest. These are very specific details based on actual, real-life places and events in Puerto Rico (such as the El Yunque forest, the 1989 Hurricane Hugo, etc.). Note also that she suggests that the main difference between the real-life events in Puerto Rico and the events in *Species* is that in the movie, the monster is killed at the end—the clear implication being that in real life the monster continues to exist in Puerto Rico.

Before I interviewed Ms. Tolentino, I was concerned that she might have seen the film *Species* after her chupacabra sighting but before her interview (for example on home video). However, I discovered through further research that this would have been impossible since VHS tapes of the film available for home viewing were not released until August 26, 1997—after the interview took place. In her 2010 interview with me, Tolentino confirmed that she had indeed seen *Species* before her sighting.

7. It is interesting, when reading reports of the chupacabra attacks and sightings, how often fictional films are mentioned in the same context. Eyewitnesses (or perhaps the reporters who interviewed them) often compared chupacabra-related phenomenon to paranormal and science-fiction films they had seen. For example, in Scott Corrales's book, one eyewitness states that strange slime found near a supposed chupacabra victim "was reminiscent of the substance made famous by the film *Ghostbusters*" (1997, 81); another writer compares the chupacabra to "*Friday the 13th* movies and the exploits of Freddy Krueger [of the *Nightmare on Elm Street* series]"; another said that a search for the chupacabra reminded him of an episode from the old *Fantasy Island* TV show (73); and so on. In my interview with Tolentino, she compared the creature she had seen to yet another famous film alien: *E.T.: The Extraterrestrial*.

Chapter 8

1. In an attempt to refute these skeptical explanations by medical professionals, Scott Corrales quotes one veterinarian, Carlos Soto, who autopsied dead rabbits, as saying, "If dogs or apes had been the culprits, there would have been the inevitable tearing of the flesh that is associated with said attacks" (Corrales 2010). In fact, Soto is simply wrong; dog bites do not "inevitably" tear flesh, and often leave clean puncture wounds, a fact easily confirmed by an Internet search for images of dog bites.

Adolfi, John. 2010. E-mail interview with the author, May 31.

Aguilar, Elvia. 2004. "Think You Can Identify This Creature?" *San Antonio Express-News*, April 29.

Altschuler, Daniel. 2005. Interview on "Chupacabra." *Is It Real?* National Geographic Television, October 12.

Anaya, Rudolfo. 2006. *Curse of the ChupaCabra*. Albuquerque: University of New Mexico Press.

———. 2008. *ChupaCabra and the Roswell UFO*. Albuquerque: University of New Mexico Press.

Animal X. 1997. "Chupacabras, Magic Cows, Black Dogs." Travel Channel. Season 1, episode 1, January 1.

Ansion, Juan. 1989. *Pishtacos de Verdugos a Sacaojos*. Lima, Peru: Asociacíaon de Publicacíones Educativas.

Armijo, Barbara. 2005. "It's Creepy, Yes, but No Chupacabra." *Rio Rancho Journal*, February 12, A-1.

Associated Press. 1996. "Farmers Blame Livestock Deaths on 'Goatsucker.'" *Albuquerque Journal*, May 7, A-2.

Ayer, Jerry. 2009. Interview by the author, September 20.

Barber, Paul. 1988. *Vampires, Burial, and Death: Folklore and Reality*. New Haven: Yale University Press.

Bartholomew, Robert. 2001. *Little Green Men, Meowing Nuns, and Head-Hunting Panics: A Study of Mass Psychogenic Illness and Social Delusion*. Jefferson, NC: McFarland and Company.

Bartholomew, Robert, and Benjamin Radford. 2003. *Hoaxes, Myths, and Manias: Why We Need Critical Thinking*. Amherst, NY: Prometheus Books.

Batson-Savage, Tanya. 2006. "Taking the Old to Tackle the New. Review of *Caribbean Mythology and Modern Life*, by Paloma Mohamed." *Sunday Gleaner* (Jamaica), November 19, F-8.

BBC News. 2009. "'Fat for Cosmetics' Murder Suspects Arrested in Peru." November 20. http://news.bbc.co.uk/2/hi/8369674.

Beresford, Matthew. 2008. *From Demons to Dracula: The Creation of the Modern Vampire Myth*. London: Reaktion Books.

Beyerstein, Barry. 2007. "Graphology—A Total Write-off." In *Tall Tales About the Mind and Brain*, edited by Sergio Dells Sala. New York: Oxford University Press.

Blackman, W. Haden. 1998. *The Field Guide to North American Monsters*. New York: Three Rivers Press.

Boie, Kevin, and Fil Alvarado. 2010. "Dead Chupacabra Lives On." Myfoxdfw.com, January 22.

Bowdenchuck, Michael. 2010. State director for the Texas Wildlife Services program. Interview by the author, January 20.

Bullard, Thomas E. 2000. "Chupacabras in Perspective." *International UFO Reporter* 25 (4): 1–30.

Cahoon, Lauren. 2008. "Hairless Hounds: Healers Too?" ABC News.com, April 11. http://abcnews.go.com/Health/PainNews/story?id=4629545&page=1&page=1.

Campion-Vincent, Veronique. 1990. "The Baby-Parts Story: A New Latin American Legend." *Western Folklore* 49:9–25.

———. 1997. "Organ Theft Narratives." *Western Folklore* 56:1–37.

Canion, Phylis. 2007a. "The Cuero Chupacabra: An Interview with Phylis Canion." Paranormal Café podcast, September 8. http://paranormalcafe.podomatic.com/entry/2007–09–08T09_06_50–07_00.

———. 2007b. "Phylis Canion's Cuero Chupacabra DNA Result." Paranormal Café podcast, November 22. http://paranormalcafe.podomatic.com/entry/2007–11–22T08_51_18–08_00.

———. 2007c. Interview by the author, December 15.

———. 2007d. E-mail interview with the author, December 31.

———. 2008. Interview by the author, January 4.

———. 2009. Message on website at www.cuerochupacabra.com, accessed September 28.

Carroll, Robert Todd. 2003. *The Skeptic's Dictionary: A Collection of Strange Beliefs, Amusing Deceptions, and Dangerous Delusions.* Hoboken, NJ: John Wiley and Sons.

Chavez, Eulogio. 1996. Personal interview by the author, May 30.

"Chupacabras Rides Agains Again." 2002a. *Fortean Times*, no. 156.

"Chupacabras Rides Again." 2002b. *Fortean Times*, no. 156.

Coleman, Loren. 2003. *Bigfoot! The True Story of Apes in America.* New York: Paraview Press.

———. 2009. Interview by the author, October 30.

———. 2010. Blog posting at Cryptomundo.com. February 5. http://www.cryptomundo.com/cryptozoo-news/island-blood/.

Coleman, Loren, and Patrick Huyghe. 1999. *The Field Guide to Bigfoot, Yeti, and Other Mystery Primates Worldwide.* New York: Avon Books.

Conger, Joe. 2007a. "Mysterious Animal Found by Cuero Rancher Identified." KENS-5 Eyewitness News, July 30. http://www.mysanantonio.com.

———. 2007b. "South Texas Rancher Finds Mysterious Animal." KENS-5 Eyewitness News, November 2. http://www.mysanantonio.com.

———. 2009. Interview by the author, October 22.

Corrales, Scott. 1996. "How Many Goats Can a Goatsucker Suck?" *Fortean Times*, no. 189, 34–37.

———. 1997. *Chupacabras and Other Mysteries.* Murfreesboro, TN: Greenleaf Publications.

———. 2010. "Night of the Chupacabras." *Inexplicata: The Journal of Hispanic UFOlogy* (blog), June 1. inexplicata.blogspot.com.

Cunliffe, Clare. 2009. Interview by the author, October 27.

Dance, Peter. 1975. *Animal Fakes and Frauds*. Avon, England: Purnell and Sons.

Derby, Lauren. 2008. "Imperial Secrets: Vampires and Nationhood in Puerto Rico." *Past and Present* 199 (suppl 3): 290–312.

Disotell, Todd. 2004. Letter to Devin McAnally. Re: Elmendorf Texas Tooth Sample DNA Analysis. Copy in author's archives.

Douglas, Jim. 2010. "Positive ID for Strange Creature in Wise County." WFAA-TV (Dallas–Fort Worth), January 19.

Downes, Jonathan. 2001. *Only Fools and Goatsuckers*. North Devon, England: Centre for Fortean Zoology Press.

———. 2008a. "Re-evaluating the Chupacabra," talk at the 2008 UnConvention. www.youtube.com/watch?v=7BK8myjdltc.

———. 2008b. *The Island of Paradise: Chupacabra, UFO Crash Retrievals and Accelerated Evolution on the Island of Puerto Rico*. North Devon, England: Centre for Fortean Zoology Press.

———. 2009. E-mail interview with the author, November 9.

Dukart, Tom. 2005. "Game and Fish: Bizarre Creature an Ocean Skate." KOB-TV (Albuquerque), February 12.

Eberhart, George. 2002. *Mysterious Creatures: A Guide to Cryptozoology*. Vol. 1. Oxford, England: ABC Clio.

Feltham, Steve. 1996. Interview by the author, April 26.

Fineman, Mark. 1996. "Tales of Bloodthirsty Beast Terrify Mexico." *Los Angeles Times*, May 19. http://articles.latimes.com/1996–05–19/news/mn-5916_1_mexico-city.

Flinter, Jorge. 1834 (2002). *An Account of the Present State of the Island of Puerto Rico*. London: Longman, Rees, Orme, Brown, Green, and Longman. Reprint, San Juan, PR: Academia Puertorriquena de la Historia.

"Florida Coyote." 2008. Entry on the website of St. Petersburg, Florida. http://www.stpete.org/wildlife/florida_coyote.asp.

Fordham, Joe. 2009. Interview by the author, September 6.

Forstner, Michael. 2007a. Posts on www.mysanantonio.com, November 2.

———. 2007b. Interview on www.mysanantonio.com, November 2.

———. 2009. Interview by the author, October 15.

Friedman, Robert. 1996. "The Chupacabra Becomes a Recurring Legend." *San Juan* (Puerto Rico) *Star*, May 6.

Garza, Xavier. 2006. *Juan and the Chupacabras*. Houston, TX: Piñata Books.

Genzmer, Herbert, and Ulrich Hellenbrand. 2007. *Mysteries of the World*. Hertsfordshire, England: Parragon Books.

Giger, H. R. 1995. *Species Design*. Beverley Hills, CA: Morpheus International.

———. 2001. *HR Giger ARH+: 30 Postcards*. London: Taschen Books.

Greste, Peter. 2000. "Experts Sink Teeth into Goat-Sucker." BBC News, September 6.

Hallcox, Jarrett, and Amy Welch. 2007. *Bodies We've Buried: Inside the National Forensic Academy, the World's Top CSI Training School*. New York: Berkley Books.

Herman, Marc. 2000. "El Chupacabra." Discovery.com. http://www.lorencoleman.com/chupacabra_1.html.

Hill, Frances. 1997. *A Delusion of Satan: The Full Story of the Salem Witch Trials*. New York: Doubleday.

Hirstein, William. 2006. *Brain Fiction: Self-Deception and the Riddle of Confabulation*. Cambridge: Massachusetts Institute of Technology.

Howe, Linda Moulton. 2009. Interview by the author, August 2.

Hufford, David. 1982. *The Terror That Comes in the Night: An Experience-centered Study of Supernatural Assault Traditions*. Philadelphia: University of Pennsylvania Press.

Is It Real? 2005. "Chupacabra." National Geographic Television, October 12.

Janis, I. L. 1963. "Group Identification under Conditions of External Danger." *British Journal of Medical Psychology* 36:227–38.

Jordan, Robert Michael. 2008. "El Chupacabra: Icon of Resistance to U.S. Imperialism." MA thesis, University of Texas at Dallas.

Knight-Ridder. 2000. "Scientist: Skeleton Not from Legendary Monster Bloodsucker." *Elyria (Ohio) Chronicle-Telegram*, September 5, D-3.

Koester, Jay. 2010. "Chicken Deaths near Horizon City Spark Talk of Chupacabras." *El Paso Times*, January 13. http://www.elpasotimes.com/ci_14172713.

Lee, Marie G. 1999. *Night of the Chupacabras*. New York: Avon Camelot.

Levy, Joel [as The Cryptozoological Society of London]. 1999. *A Natural History of the Unnatural World*. New York: St. Martin's Press.

Lloyd, James. 2001. *Chupacabras: The Devil's Genetics*. Jacksonville, OR: Christian Media.

Loftus, Elizabeth. 1980. *Memory*. New York: Addison-Wesley.

Loxton, Daniel. 2007. "Something's Saving Lee Straw's Sheep." Post on Cryptomundo. com, June 9. http://www.cryptomundo.com/cryptozoo-news/straw-sheep/#comment-31570.

———. 2009. "The Shocking Secret of Thetis Lake." *Junior Skeptic*, no. 35.

Lundborg, Pam. 2009. "'Chupacabra' Remains Bought by Oswego County Man." *Syracuse Post-Standard*, September 25. http://www.syracuse.com/news/index.ssf/2009/09/chupacabra_remains_bought_by_o.html.

Maestas, Tim. 2007. "Spooky Critter Conjures Chupacabra." KRQE News, Albuquerque, New Mexico. Airdate November 8.

Mangum, James A., and Sidney Spires. 2008. *The Fairy and the Chupacabra and Those Marfa Lights*. Houston, TX: John M. Hardy Publishing.

McAnally, Devin. 2009a. "The Elmendorf Chupacabra Story." September 19. http://www.texasbluedog.org/index.html.

———. 2009b. Interview by the author, November 9.

McLeod, Michael. 2009. *Anatomy of a Beast: Obsession and Myth on the Trail of Bigfoot*. Berkeley: University of California Press.

Métraux, Alfred. 1959. *Voodoo in Haiti*. London: Schocken Books.

Miller, Bill. 2010. "Biologist: Texas 'Chupacabra' a Hairless Raccoon." (Fort Worth) *Star-Telegram*, January 22. http://www.star-telegram.com/668/story/1914526.html.

Mohamed, Paloma. 2003. *Caribbean Mythology and Modern Life: Five One-Act Plays for Young People*. Dover, MA: Majority Press.

Montes, Lucas. 2010. Interview by the author, May 31.

Navarro, Mireya. 1996. "Animals Killed, an Island Is Abuzz." *New York Times*, January 26.

Nickell, Joe. 1996. "Goatsucker Hysteria." *Skeptical Inquirer*, September/October, 12.

O'Neill, Terry. 2007. *Chupacabra*. Farmington Hills, MI: Kidhaven Press.

Pierce, Tony. 2009. "Is That a Chupacabra Being Stuffed by a Taxidermist in Texas?" *Los Angeles Times*, September 2. http://latimesblogs.latimes.com/unleashed/2009/09/chupacabra-found-and-stuffed-by-taxidermist-in-texas.html.

Pilkington, Mark. 2000. "Chupacabras Fever." *Fortean Times*, no. 140, 22–23.

Plá, Lucy. 1996. "Los Chupacabras: The Interview–Part 1." March 20. http://www.ufodigest.com/chupa.html.

Power, Matthew. 2006. "Exploring Nicaragua's Forgotten Passage." *National Geographic Explorer*, September, 80–85.

Radford, Benjamin. 1996. "Lik'ichiri: Menace or Myth?" *Bolivian Times*, May 9.

———. 1999. "Bitter Harvest: The Organ-Snatching Urban Legends." *Skeptical Inquirer* 23 (3) (May/June): 34–39.

———. 2006. "Mystery Monster Dogs Maine." Bad Science column, LiveScience.com, September 24. http://www.livescience.com/strangenews/060924_maine_monster.html.

———. 2007. "Chupacabras of the Southwest." (Albuquerque) *Weekly Alibi*, November 15–21.

———. 2008. "Popobawa." *Fortean Times*, no. 241. November.

———. 2009. "Return of the Montauk Monster: Same Ol' Myth?" Bad Science column, LiveScience.com, May 14. http://www.livescience.com/strangenews/090514-montauk-monster.html.

———. 2010a. "New Chupacabra Revealed as Montauk Monster." Bad Science column, LiveScience.com, January 20. http://www.livescience.com/strangenews/etc/100120-new-chupacabra-revealed-montauk-monster.html.

———. 2010b. "Tracking the Goat Sucker." *Fortean Times*, no. 257 (January): 48–53.

———. 2010c. "Belief in Magic, Witchcraft Widespread in Africa." Bad Science column, LiveScience.com. August 30. http://www.livescience.com/strangenews/belief-witchcraft-magic-widespread-africa-100830.html.

———. 2010d. "Yeti and Other Mangy Monster Sightings on the Rise." Bad Science column, LiveScience.com, August 30. http://www.livescience.com/strangenews/yeti-mangy-monster-sightings.html.

———. 2010e. *Scientific Paranormal Investigation: How to Solve Unexplained Mysteries*. Albuquerque, NM: Rhombus Publishing Company.

Radford, Benjamin, and Joe Nickell. 2007. *Lake Monster Mysteries: Investigating the World's Most Elusive Creatures*. Lexington: University Press of Kentucky.

Ramsland, Katherine. 2002. *The Science of Vampires*. New York: Penguin Putnam.

Reed, Taren. 2010. "Is the Legendary Beast Killing Texas Farmer's Chickens?" (Jacksonville, FL) *First Coast News*, January 15.

Rigau-Perez, J. G., A. V. Vorndam, and G. G. Clark. 2001. "The Dengue and Dengue Hemorrhagic Fever Epidemic in Puerto Rico, 1994–1995." *American Journal of Medicine* 64 (1–2): 67–74.

Roach, Marilynne K. 2002. *The Salem Witch Trials: A Day-by-Day Chronicle of a Community Under Siege*. New York: Cooper Square Press.

Royte, Elizabeth. 2010. "Canis Soup." *Outside*, March.

Sabbagh, Karl. 2009. *Remembering Our Childhood: How Memory Betrays Us*. New York: Oxford University Press.

Shapiro, Marc. 1995a. "Breeding New Species." *Fangoria*, no. 143 (June): 20–25.

———. 1995b. "Supervising Species." *Fangoria*, no. 144 (July): 26–31.

Shay, Estelle. 1995. "Capturing an Alien Species." *Cinefex*, no. 63 (September): 39–40, 45–48.

Shermer, Michael. 1997. *Why People Believe Weird Things*. New York: MJF Books.

Shuker, Karl P. N. 2009a. *The Unexplained*. New York: Metro Books.

———. 2009b. E-mail interview with the author, May 19.

Sparrow, Giles. 2009. *Field Guide to Fantastic Creatures*. London: Querus Publishing, Inc.

Species press kit. 1995. MGM Studios.

Speers-Roesch, Benjamin. 2010. Interview by the author, June 8.

Stein, Gordon. 1996. "Vampire." In *The Encyclopedia of the Paranormal*. Buffalo, NY: Prometheus Books.

Stewart, James. 1977. "Cattle Mutilations: An Episode of Collective Delusion." *The Zetetic* 1 (2): 55–66.

Taub, Sheila, ed. 1999. *Recovered Memories of Child Sexual Abuse*. Springfield, IL: Charles C. Thomas Publishers.

"This Isn't My Goatsucker! Farmer Says Skeletons Were Switched." 2000. *La Prensa de Nicaragua*, September 5.

Tolentino, Madelyne. 2010. Interview by the author, June 18.

Trainor, Joseph. 1997. "Chupacabras Scare Sweeps Brazil." *UFO Roundup* 2 (20), May 18. http://www.ufoinfo.com/roundup/vo2/rndo2_20.shtml#1.

UnexplainedStuff.com. 2008. "Creatures of the Night: Chupacabra." http://www.unexplainedstuff.com/Mysterious-Creatures/Creatures-of-the-Night-Chupacabra.html.

Upton, Reed. 2005. "Strange Corpse Has Some Muttering the Word 'Chupacabra.'" KOB-TV (Albuquerque), February 10.

Valdez, Carlos. 1997. Interview on *Animal X*, 1997.

Vaughn, Lewis. 2008. *The Power of Critical Thinking*. 2nd ed. New York: Oxford University Press.

Vergara, Marianela Flores. 2000. "The Church Gets Involved." *El Nuevo Diaria* (Nicaragua), September 1.

Wachtel, Nathan. 1994. *Gods and Vampires: Return to Chipaya*. Translated by Carol Volk. Chicago: University of Chicago Press.

Wade, Dale A., and James E. Bowns. 1984. *Procedures for Evaluating Predation on Livestock and Wildlife*. Document B-1429. College Station: Texas A&M University System and U.S. Fish and Wildlife Service, Department of the Interior.

Wade, Kimberley A., Sarah L. Green, and Robert A. Nash. 2009. "Can Fabricated Evidence Induce False Eyewitness Testimony?" *Applied Cognitive Psychology*. Wiley InterScience, www.interscience.wiley.com. doi:10.1002/acp.1607.

Wagner, Lloyd S. 2004. *El Chupacabras: Trail of the Goatsucker*. Bloomington, IN: Iuniverse.

White, Luise. 2000. *Speaking with Vampires: Rumor and History in Colonial Africa*. Berkeley: University of California Press.

Woodward, Ian. 1979. *The Werewolf Delusion*. London: Paddington Press.

Ynurreta, Francisco. 2008. "Chupacabras Reappears in Champotón, Campeche, Mexico; It Kills 9 Birds." *El Universal* (Mexico City), April 4.

Index